To: _____

From: _____

Your word is a lamp to my feet
  and a light for my path, O LORD.

Psalm 119:105

God's Words of Life for Students
Copyright 2001 by Zondervan
ISBN 0-310-98414-9

All devotions taken from *The Student Bible, New International Version,* © 1986, 1992, 1996 by The Zondervan Corporation. Notes by Philip Yancey and Tim Stafford. (Grand Rapids, Michigan: ZondervanPublishingHouse, 1996).

Requests for information should be addressed to:
    Inspirio, The gift group of Zondervan
    Grand Rapids, Michigan 49530
    http://www.inspiriogifts.com

Associate Editor: Molly C. Detweiler
Cover and Interior Design: Amy E. Langeler
Compiler: Emily Klotz

Printed in China

02 03 04 / HK / 4 3 2 1

GOD'S WORDS OF LIFE FOR
STUDENTS

from the
New
International
Version

inspirio
The gift group of Zondervan

Table of Contents

GOD'S WORDS OF LIFE ON

Attitude....................................6
Beliefs 10
Courage..................................14
Decisions 18
Difficult Times 22
Doubts 28
Emotions 32
Encouragement 36
Faith......................................40
Family 44
Forgiveness.............................48
Friends 52
Future Plans............................56
God's Grace.............................62
God's Will...............................66
Growth 70
Guidance................................74
Heaven 78
Hope 84
Identity..................................90
Joy 96
Knowledge 102

Loneliness 106
Love 110
Money 116
Patience 120
Peace...124
Perseverance....................................130
Praise and Worship 134
Prayer..138
Priorities 144
Protection 148
Relationships....................................152
Rest 156
Sharing Your Faith............................162
Strength 166
Stress 172
Talents and Abilities 176
Temptation.......................................180
Trust 184
Wisdom 190
Words 196
Work 200
Worry...204

ATTITUDE

Be imitators of God, therefore, as dearly loved children and live a life of love, just as Christ loved us and gave himself up for us as a fragrant offering and sacrifice to God.

Ephesians 5:1–2

Rejoice in the Lord always. I will say it again: Rejoice! Let your gentleness be evident to all. The Lord is near. Do not be anxious about anything, but in everything, by prayer and petition, with thanksgiving, present your requests to God. And the peace of God, which transcends all understanding, will guard your hearts and your minds in Christ Jesus.

Philippians 4:4–7

Do to others as you would have them do to you. … Love your enemies, do good to them, and lend to them without expecting to get anything back. Then your reward will be great, and you will be sons of the Most High.

Luke 6:31, 35

A generous man will himself be blessed,
   for he shares his food with the poor.

Proverbs 22:9

Blessed are the merciful,
for they will be shown mercy.

Matthew 5:7

Let us not become weary in doing good, for at
the proper time we will reap a harvest if we do
not give up. Therefore, as we have opportunity,
let us do good to all people, especially to
those who belong to the family of believers.

Galatians 6:9–10

Your attitude should be the same as that of
Christ Jesus:
Who, being in very nature God,
did not consider equality with God
something to be grasped,
but made himself nothing,
taking the very nature of a servant,
being made in human likeness.
And being found in appearance as a man,
he humbled himself
and became obedient to death—
even death on a cross!
Therefore God exalted him to the highest place
and gave him the name that is above every
name.

Philippians 2:5–9

ATTITUDE

Jesus called a little child and had him stand among them.... Jesus said, "Whoever humbles himself like this child is the greatest in the kingdom of heaven."

Matthew 18:2, 4

If you really keep the royal law found in Scripture, "Love your neighbor as yourself," you are doing right.

James 2:8

As God's chosen people, holy and dearly loved, clothe yourselves with compassion, kindness, humility, gentleness and patience. Bear with each other and forgive whatever grievances you may have against one another. Forgive as the Lord forgave you. And over all these virtues put on love, which binds them all together in perfect unity.

Colossians 3:12–14

Whoever exalts himself will be humbled, and whoever humbles himself will be exalted.

Matthew 23:12

Attitude

Mary and Martha both had a close relationship with Jesus, who loved them deeply. He visited the sisters' home three times that we know of, and probably many more. Like many sisters, Mary and Martha had quite different personalities, and we can see the difference clearly in how they related to Jesus.

Mary could drop everything and listen to Jesus. When he called, she answered instantly. She showed her love for him in extravagant ways, once lavishing a huge amount of expensive perfume on his feet (John 12:3). For Mary, everything stopped when Jesus was present.

Mary's ways sometimes annoyed Martha, who showed more obsessive concern about getting things done. "Duty first" was Martha's motto. She served Jesus by preparing meals and doing the work of hosting.

Which way was better? Martha preferred her own hard-working style, and she asked Jesus to set Mary straight. Jesus gently disagreed. Mary, who simply sat at his feet and listened, did the one really necessary thing in life, he said, and he would not reprove her (Luke 10:41–42).

GOD'S WORDS OF LIFE ON
BELIEFS

God so loved the world that he gave his one and only Son, that whoever believes in him shall not perish but have eternal life.

John 3:16

Jesus said, "If anyone is thirsty, let him come to me and drink. Whoever believes in me, as the Scripture has said, streams of living water will flow from within him."

John 7:37–38

Jesus cried out, "When a man believes in me, he does not believe in me only, but in the one who sent me. When he looks at me, he sees the one who sent me. I have come into the world as a light, so that no one who believes in me should stay in darkness."

John 12:44–46

Jesus said, "Whoever acknowledges me before men, I will also acknowledge him before my Father in heaven."

Matthew 10:32

BELIEFS

Like newborn babies, crave pure spiritual milk, so that by it you may grow up in your salvation, now that you have tasted that the Lord is good.

1 Peter 2:2–3

Just as you received Christ Jesus as Lord, continue to live in him, rooted and built up in him, strengthened in the faith as you were taught, and overflowing with thankfulness.

Colossians 2:6–7

It is God who makes both us and you stand firm in Christ. He anointed us, set his seal of ownership on us, and put his Spirit in our hearts as a deposit, guaranteeing what is to come.

2 Corinthians 1:21–22

If you believe, you will receive whatever you ask for in prayer.

Matthew 21:22

To all who received Christ, to those who believed in his name, he gave the right to become children of God.

John 1:12

BELIEFS

"See, I lay a stone in Zion,
    a chosen and precious cornerstone,
and the one who trusts in him
    will never be put to shame," says the Lord.

1 Peter 2:6

Jesus declared, "I am the bread of life. He who comes to me will never go hungry, and he who believes in me will never be thirsty."

John 6:35

Everything is possible for him who believes.

Mark 9:23

Jesus told Thomas, "Because you have seen me, you have believed; blessed are those who have not seen and yet have believed."

John 20:29

BELIEFS

Most of Jesus' disciples were ordinary people with no status to worry about losing. A fisherman or tax collector would not forfeit much if he followed an unorthodox teacher. In contrast, Nicodemus had quite a reputation at stake. As a member of the Jewish Sanhedrin, he held an important ruling post. As a Pharisee, he was committed to a certain set of beliefs.

No doubt that is why Nicodemus first asked Jesus to meet him at night. As time went on, however, Nicodemus grew more bold. When the Sanhedrin discussed Jesus, he spoke out against their willingness to condemn the man without talking to him (John 7:50–52).

After Jesus' death, Nicodemus let his sentiments become more public. Along with Joseph of Arimathea, he took Jesus' body from Calvary and prepared it for burial.

The Bible tells us no more about Nicodemus, so we can't be sure whether he ever openly confessed faith in Jesus. It seems likely, however, that John mentions these incidents because Nicodemus was willing to talk to John about what he believed. John's Gospel gives reason to hope that Nicodemus sacrificed his reputation—and gained a new birth—in the end.

COURAGE

I can do everything through Christ who gives me strength.

Philippians 4:13

"Do not fear, for I am with you;
   do not be dismayed, for I am your God.
I will strengthen you and help you;
   I will uphold you with my righteous right
hand," declares the LORD.

Isaiah 41:10

[A righteous man] will have no fear of bad news;
   his heart is steadfast, trusting in the LORD.

Psalm 112:7

Be strong and courageous. Do not be terrified;
do not be discouraged, for the LORD your God
will be with you wherever you go.

Joshua 1:9

This is what the LORD says—
   he who created you, O Jacob,
   he who formed you, O Israel:
"Fear not, for I have redeemed you;
   I have summoned you by name; you are mine."

Isaiah 43:1

The LORD gives strength to the weary
and increases the power of the weak.

Isaiah 40:29

In Christ and through faith in him we may
approach God with freedom and confidence.

Ephesians 3:12

The righteous cry out, and the LORD hears them;
he delivers them from all their troubles.

Psalm 34:17

Jesus said, "Peace I leave with you; my peace
I give you. I do not give to you as the world
gives. Do not let your hearts be troubled and
do not be afraid."

John 14:27

Though I walk in the midst of trouble,
you preserve my life, O LORD;
you stretch out your hand against the anger
of my foes,
with your right hand you save me.

Psalm 138:7

COURAGE

Be strong and take heart,
all you who hope in the LORD.

Psalm 31:24

Do not throw away your confidence; it will be richly rewarded. You need to persevere so that when you have done the will of God, you will receive what he has promised.

Hebrews 10:35–36

The LORD is my light and my salvation—
whom shall I fear?
The LORD is the stronghold of my life—
of whom shall I be afraid?

Psalm 27:1

I am still confident of this:
I will see the goodness of the LORD
in the land of the living.
Wait for the LORD;
be strong and take heart
and wait for the LORD.

Psalm 27:13–14

COURAGE

Few scenes in the Bible are more dramatic than the one in 1 Kings 18. The forces of evil and good collided head-on. On that day, a bedraggled desert prophet single-handedly took on a king and nearly a thousand powerful priests.

Israel was at a crossroads. Other kings had introduced idolatry into Israelite religion, but King Ahab and the notorious Queen Jezebel were going much further. They wanted to wipe out all worship of the true God.

The prophet Elijah proved a worthy adversary. His very name meant "The LORD is my God." He proposed a showdown, the ultimate contest to prove who was the true God. First Kings presents the scene in full color, complete with the priests' desperate contortions and Elijah's mocking, taunting commentary. In the final analysis, it was no contest at all. God unleashed a spectacular display of raw power.

Elijah was one of the most colorful of all Israel's prophets. He suffered from bouts of depression and self-doubt, but during times of crisis he showed amazing courage. The Mount Carmel showdown was merely one example of that courage.

DECISIONS

Trust in the LORD with all your heart
    and lean not on your own understanding;
in all your ways acknowledge him,
    and he will make your paths straight.

Proverbs 3:5–6

Your word is a lamp to my feet
    and a light for my path, O LORD.

Psalm 119:105

The LORD guides me in paths of righteousness
    for his name's sake.

Psalm 23:3

When he, the Spirit of truth, comes, he will guide you into all truth. He will not speak on his own; he will speak only what he hears, and he will tell you what is yet to come.

John 16:13

"I will instruct you and teach you
    in the way you should go;
I will counsel you and watch over you," says the LORD.

Psalm 32:8

If any of you lacks wisdom, he should ask God, who gives generously to all without finding fault, and it will be given to him.

James 1:5

Delight yourself in the LORD
and he will give you the desires of your heart.
Commit your way to the LORD;
trust in him and he will do this:
He will make your righteousness shine like the dawn,
the justice of your cause like the noonday sun.
Be still before the LORD *and wait patiently for him.*

Psalm 37:4–7

Do not conform any longer to the pattern of this world, but be transformed by the renewing of your mind. Then you will be able to test and approve what God's will is—his good, pleasing and perfect will.

Romans 12:2

You guide me with your counsel,
and afterward you will take me into glory, O God.

Psalm 73:24

DECISIONS

Whether you turn to the right or to the left, your ears will hear a voice behind you, saying, "This is the way; walk in it."

Isaiah 30:21

The LORD *will guide you always.*

Isaiah 58:11

For lack of guidance a nation falls,
but many advisers make victory sure.

Proverbs 11:14

Do not be anxious about anything, but in everything, by prayer and petition, with thanksgiving, present your requests to God. And the peace of God, which transcends all understanding, will guard your hearts and your minds in Christ Jesus.

Philippians 4:6–7

DECISIONS

Proverbs is probably the most down-to-earth book in the Bible. The book offers the warm advice you get by growing up in a good family: practical guidance for making successful decisions. Some of the advice in Proverbs seems particularly well suited to young people: warnings against joining gangs, for instance, or urgent cautions against sex outside of marriage. But the central message of Proverbs applies to anyone, old or young: "Get wisdom at all costs."

Proverbs simply tells how life works most of the time. The godly, moral, hardworking, and wise will reap many rewards. Fools and scoffers, though they appear successful, will eventually pay the cost of their lifestyle. Proverbs frankly concedes that the wise path will not be chosen by many. It is easier to live carelessly, but choices that seem perfectly right may end up destroying you. However, those who choose to live by Proverbs will get success and safety, and more. They will get to know God himself. "Then you will understand the fear of the LORD and find the knowledge of God" (Proverbs 2:5).

DIFFICULT TIMES

"When you pass through the waters,
    I will be with you;
and when you pass through the rivers,
    they will not sweep over you.
When you walk through the fire,
    you will not be burned;
    the flames will not set you ablaze," says the LORD.

Isaiah 43:2

The LORD is good,
    a refuge in times of trouble.
He cares for those who trust in him.

Nahum 1:7

The LORD gives sight to the blind,
the LORD lifts up those who are bowed down,
    the LORD loves the righteous.

Psalm 146:8

A righteous man may have many troubles,
    but the LORD delivers him from them all.

Psalm 34:19

My flesh and my heart may fail,
    but God is the strength of my heart
    and my portion forever.

Psalm 73:26

DIFFICULT TIMES

Why are you downcast, O my soul?
  Why so disturbed within me?
Put your hope in God,
  for I will yet praise him,
  my Savior and my God.

Psalm 42:11

If you make the Most High your dwelling—
  even the LORD, who is my refuge—
then no harm will befall you,
  no disaster will come near your tent.
For he will command his angels concerning you
  to guard you in all your ways;
they will lift you up in their hands,
  so that you will not strike your foot against a stone.

Psalm 91:9–12

Those who sow in tears
  will reap with songs of joy.
He who goes out weeping,
  carrying seed to sow,
will return with songs of joy,
  carrying sheaves with him.

Psalm 126:5–6

DIFFICULT TIMES

You are my hiding place, O LORD;
  you will protect me from trouble
  and surround me with songs of deliverance.

Psalm 32:7

Jesus said, "In this world you will have trouble. But take heart! I have overcome the world."

John 16:33

The LORD is my rock, my fortress and my deliverer;
  my God is my rock, in whom I take refuge.
  He is my shield and the horn of my salvation,
  my stronghold.

Psalm 18:2

The LORD himself goes before you and will be with you; he will never leave you nor forsake you. Do not be afraid; do not be discouraged.

Deuteronomy 31:8

Praise be to the God and Father of our Lord Jesus Christ, the Father of compassion and the God of all comfort, who comforts us in all our troubles, so that we can comfort those in any trouble with the comfort we ourselves have received from God.

2 Corinthians 1:3–4

DIFFICULT TIMES

For Christ's sake, I delight in weaknesses, in insults, in hardships, in persecutions, in difficulties. For when I am weak, then I am strong.

2 Corinthians 12:10

Is anything too hard for the LORD?

Genesis 18:14

With God all things are possible.

Matthew 19:26

I can do everything through Christ who gives me strength.

Philippians 4:13

The Lord knows how to rescue godly men from trials.

2 Peter 2:9

Dear friends, do not be surprised at the painful trial you are suffering, as though something strange were happening to you. But rejoice that you participate in the sufferings of Christ, so that you may be overjoyed when his glory is revealed. If you are insulted because of the name of Christ, you are blessed, for the Spirit of glory and of God rests on you.

1 Peter 4:12–14

25

DIFFICULT TIMES

Blessed is the man who perseveres under trial, because when he has stood the test, he will receive the crown of life that God has promised to those who love him.

James 1:12

Consider it pure joy ... whenever you face trials of many kinds, because you know that the testing of your faith develops perseverance.

James 1:2–3

Who shall separate us from the love of Christ? Shall trouble or hardship or persecution or famine or nakedness or danger or sword? ... No, in all these things we are more than conquerors through him who loved us.

Romans 8:35, 37

DIFFICULT TIMES

"I consider that our present sufferings are not worth comparing with the glory that will be revealed in us" (Romans 8:18). Paul never minimizes suffering: after all, his own life included beatings, imprisonment, shipwrecks, assassination attempts, and chronic illness. But he insists with absolute conviction that future rewards will outweigh all present sufferings.

Olympic athletes endure years of eight-hour practice sessions and much discipline and pain for the goal of winning a gold medal. Similarly, the Christian's life on earth may involve many difficulties (Romans 8:22–23), but the end result will make them seem worthwhile.

"And we know that in all things God works for the good of those who love him, who have been called according to his purpose" (Romans 8:28). This famous verse is often misquoted or stretched to mean more than it says. Paul doesn't promise that only good, or pleasurable, things will come to the Christian. What he does say is that even the difficult experiences described in verses 35–39 can be used in God's overall plan for good. And nothing can separate us from the love of God.

DOUBTS

In Christ and through faith in him we may approach God with freedom and confidence.

Ephesians 3:12

God who began a good work in you will carry it on to completion until the day of Christ Jesus.

Philippians 1:6

"Though the mountains be shaken
    and the hills be removed,
yet my unfailing love for you will not be shaken
    nor my covenant of peace be removed,"
    says the LORD, *who has compassion on you.*

Isaiah 54:10

Without weakening in his faith, Abraham faced the fact that his body was as good as dead—since he was about a hundred years old—and that Sarah's womb was also dead. Yet he did not waver through unbelief regarding the promise of God, but was strengthened in his faith and gave glory to God, being fully persuaded that God had power to do what he had promised.

Romans 4:19–21

DOUBTS

Blessed is the man who trusts in the LORD,
   whose confidence is in him.

Jeremiah 17:7

Dear children, continue in Jesus, so that
when he appears we may be confident and
unashamed before him at his coming.

1 *John* 2:28

If any of you lacks wisdom, he should ask God,
who gives generously to all without finding
fault, and it will be given to him.

James 1:5

Jesus said, "I tell you the truth, if anyone says
to this mountain, 'Go, throw yourself into
the sea,' and does not doubt in his heart but
believes that what he says will happen, it will
be done for him. Therefore I tell you, whatever
you ask for in prayer, believe that you have
received it, and it will be yours."

Mark 11:23–24

DOUBTS

Let us draw near to God with a sincere heart in full assurance of faith, having our hearts sprinkled to cleanse us from a guilty conscience and having our bodies washed with pure water. Let us hold unswervingly to the hope we profess, for he who promised is faithful.

Hebrews 10:22–23

In Christ we were also chosen, having been predestined according to the plan of him who works out everything in conformity with the purpose of his will, in order that we, who were the first to hope in Christ, might be for the praise of his glory. And you also were included in Christ when you heard the word of truth, the gospel of your salvation. Having believed, you were marked in him with a seal, the promised Holy Spirit, who is a deposit guaranteeing our inheritance until the redemption of those who are God's possession—to the praise of his glory.

Ephesians 1:11–14

DOUBTS

Between stubborn skepticism and honest questioning there is a huge gap, and the disciple named Thomas illustrates the difference. Popularly known as "Doubting Thomas," this disciple stands out for his practical honesty, not for his unbelief.

Thomas never pretended. If he didn't understand something, he said so; if he felt discouraged, he acted like it.

Thomas got his reputation as a doubter primarily because of his reaction when told of Jesus' resurrection. He simply insisted, "I need to see it for myself." The implications of a risen Jesus were too great, he believed, to take someone else's word for it. Jesus honored this honest doubt, and when he visited Thomas in person to offer proof, Thomas responded with the ultimate statement of faith: "My Lord and my God" (John 20:28). He was, in fact, the only disciple who specifically addressed Jesus as God.

Thomas's questions led to faith because he expressed them sincerely and looked for answers.

EMOTIONS

May the righteous be glad
   and rejoice before God;
   may they be happy and joyful.

Psalm 68:3

Weeping may remain for a night,
   but rejoicing comes in the morning.

Psalm 30:5

The Spirit of the Sovereign LORD is on me,
   because the LORD has anointed me
   to . . . provide for those who grieve in Zion—
to bestow on them a crown of beauty
   instead of ashes,
the oil of gladness
   instead of mourning,
and a garment of praise
   instead of a spirit of despair.

Isaiah 61:1, 3

God heals the brokenhearted
   and binds up their wounds.

Psalm 147:3

EMOTIONS

Jesus said, "You will grieve, but your grief will turn to joy. . . . Now is your time of grief, but I will see you again and you will rejoice, and no one will take away your joy."

John 16:20, 22

In your anger do not sin;
when you are on your beds,
search your hearts and be silent.

Psalm 4:4

The LORD is close to the brokenhearted
and saves those who are crushed in spirit.

Psalm 34:18

Do not fret because of evil men
or be envious of those who do wrong;
for like the grass they will soon wither,
like green plants they will soon die away.

Psalm 37:1–2

When anxiety was great within me,
your consolation brought joy to my soul,
O LORD.

Psalm 94:19

EMOTIONS

You turned my wailing into dancing;
  you removed my sackcloth
  and clothed me with joy,
that my heart may sing to you and not be silent.
  O LORD my God, I will give you thanks forever.

Psalm 30:11–12

A happy heart makes the face cheerful.

Proverbs 15:13

Is anyone happy? Let him sing songs of praise.

James 5:13

In my distress I called to the LORD;
  I cried to my God for help.
From his temple he heard my voice;
  my cry came before him, into his ears.

Psalm 18:6

EMOTIONS

Superficially, the Old Testament can sometimes read like it's taken from old movies. The good guys are the Israelites, and they fight with the bad guys from nations around them. The ending is always happy. God is on their side.

Yet, in Psalm 22 and a few other places, the "good guy" story doesn't fit at all. This poem, credited to king David, tells of tremendous suffering with no relief from God. It sounds like a mob scene, a lynching. The good guy's enemies have him. They surround him, jeering, like a pack of dogs. He is helpless and exhausted. All he can do is cry to God.

The psalmist wavers back and forth, first crying out in misery, then taking stock of God's wonderful character, then describing his misery again. The whole poem is a prayer to God. Although this cry has gone up day and night (verse 2), God remains silent.

Then, at verse 22, the poem takes a dramatic turn, switching from grief to jubilation. Somehow, God has saved the sufferer, who, in great excitement, tells others about it.

ENCOURAGEMENT

May our Lord Jesus Christ himself and God our Father, who loved us and by his grace gave us eternal encouragement and good hope, encourage your hearts and strengthen you in every good deed and word.

2 Thessalonians 2:16–17

Everything that was written in the past was written to teach us, so that through endurance and the encouragement of the Scriptures we might have hope.

Romans 15:4

Because God wanted to make the unchanging nature of his purpose very clear to the heirs of what was promised, he confirmed it with an oath. God did this so that, by two unchange-able things in which it is impossible for God to lie, we who have fled to take hold of the hope offered to us may be greatly encouraged. We have this hope as an anchor for the soul, firm and secure.

Hebrews 6:17–19

ENCOURAGEMENT

You hear, O LORD, *the desire of the afflicted;*
you encourage them, and you listen to their cry.

Psalm 10:17

Let us not give up meeting together, as some
are in the habit of doing, but let us encourage
one another.

Hebrews 10:25

O LORD, *when you favored me,*
you made my mountain stand firm.

Psalm 30:7

Be strong and take heart,
all you who hope in the LORD.

Psalm 31:24

My purpose is that they may be encouraged in
heart and united in love, so that they may have
the full riches of complete understanding, in
order that they may know the mystery of God,
namely, Christ.

Colossians 2:2

ENCOURAGEMENT

May the God who gives endurance and encouragement give you a spirit of unity among yourselves as you follow Christ Jesus.

Romans 15:5

Encourage one another daily.

Hebrews 3:13

*You are a shield around me, O L*ORD*;*
you bestow glory on me and lift up my head.

Psalm 3:3

I lift up my eyes to the hills—
where does my help come from?
*My help comes from the L*ORD*,*
the Maker of heaven and earth.
He will not let your foot slip—
he who watches over you will not slumber;
indeed, he who watches over Israel
will neither slumber nor sleep.

Psalm 121:1–4

ENCOURAGEMENT

T hough his real name was Joseph, he became known as "Barnabas," an apt nickname meaning "Son of Encouragement." Barnabas had a knack for recognizing and encouraging others' potential. His most notable beneficiary? None other than the apostle Paul.

Even after his dramatic conversion, Paul frightened Jewish Christians—so much that when he reached Jerusalem, they all kept their distance. Wasn't this the fire-breather who had hurt so many believers? But Barnabas took his life into his hands and went to see Paul. Convinced that his conversion was genuine, Barnabas led Paul to the apostles and introduced them (Acts 9:26–27).

When the first Gentile church sprang to life in Antioch, Barnabas encouraged these new Christians and then thought of a role for Paul (Acts 11:25–26). Barnabas helped Paul find his real calling: to nurture churches that crossed Jewish-Gentile lines.

FAITH

It is by grace you have been saved, through faith
—and this not from yourselves, it is the gift of
God—not by works, so that no one can boast.

Ephesians 2:8–9

Now faith is being sure of what we hope for
and certain of what we do not see.

Hebrews 11:1

This is the victory that has overcome the world,
even our faith.

1 John 5:4

A woman who had been subject to bleeding
for twelve years came up behind Jesus and
touched the edge of his cloak. She said to herself, "If I only touch his cloak, I will be healed."
Jesus turned and saw her. "Take heart, daughter,"
he said, "your faith has healed you." And the
woman was healed from that moment.

Matthew 9:20–22

In the gospel a righteousness from God is
revealed, a righteousness that is by faith from
first to last, just as it is written: "The righteous
will live by faith."

Romans 1:17

FAITH

"Have faith in God," Jesus [said]. "I tell you the truth, if anyone says to this mountain, 'Go, throw yourself into the sea,' and does not doubt in his heart but believes that what he says will happen, it will be done for him. Therefore I tell you, whatever you ask for in prayer, believe that you have received it, and it will be yours."

Mark 11:22–24

Jesus said, "I tell you the truth, anyone who has faith in me will do what I have been doing. He will do even greater things than these, because I am going to the Father. And I will do whatever you ask in my name, so that the Son may bring glory to the Father. You may ask me for anything in my name, and I will do it."

John 14:12–14

The righteousness from God comes through faith in Jesus Christ to all who believe.

Romans 3:22

Faith comes from hearing the message, and the message is heard through the word of Christ.

Romans 10:17

We live by faith, not by sight.

2 Corinthians 5:7

41

GOD'S WORDS OF LIFE ON
FAITH

You are all sons of God through faith in Christ
Jesus.

Galatians 3:26

The only thing that counts is faith expressing
itself through love.

Galatians 5:6

Take up the shield of faith, with which you can
extinguish all the flaming arrows of the evil one.

Ephesians 6:16

We always thank God, the Father of our Lord
Jesus Christ, when we pray for you, because we
have heard of your faith in Christ Jesus and of
the love you have for all the saints—the faith
and love that spring from the hope that is stored
up for you in heaven and that you have already
heard about in the word of truth, the gospel.

Colossians 1:3–5

We ought always to thank God for you, brothers,
and rightly so, because your faith is growing
more and more, and the love every one of you
has for each other is increasing.

2 Thessalonians 1:3

FAITH

What is faith? And how can you be sure you've got it? What are signs of true faith? The author of Hebrews launches into a detailed description of faith, complete with references to several dozen biographical models. (Some have dubbed Hebrews 11 as the "Faith Hall of Fame.") "Without faith," Hebrews says bluntly, "it is impossible to please God" (11:6).

The picture of faith emerging from these chapters contains some surprises. The author uses words and phrases like "persevere," "endure," "do not lose heart." In many instances, the heroes cited did not even receive the promise they hoped for.

Faith, concludes the author, most resembles a difficult race. The runner has his or her eyes on the winner's prize, and, despite nagging temptations to slacken the pace, refuses to let up until he or she crosses the finish line.

The faith described in Hebrews is not sugar-coated; God does not guarantee a life of luxury and ease. It is tough faith: a constant commitment to hang on and believe God against all odds, no matter what.

FAMILY

The *father of a righteous man has great joy;*
   he who has a wise son delights in him.
May *your father and mother be glad;*
   may she who gave you birth rejoice!

Proverbs 23:24–25

Children's *children are a crown to the aged,*
   and parents are the pride of their children.

Proverbs 17:6

Children, obey your parents in the Lord, for this is right. "Honor your father and mother"—which is the first commandment with a promise—"that it may go well with you and that you may enjoy long life on the earth.

Ephesians 6:1–3

Both the one who makes men holy and those who are made holy are of the same family. So Jesus is not ashamed to call them brothers.

Hebrews 2:11

God *sets the lonely in families.*

Psalm 68:6

FAMILY

How great is the love the Father has lavished on us, that we should be called children of God! And that is what we are!

1 John 3:1

We have all had human fathers who disciplined us and we respected them for it. How much more should we submit to the Father of our spirits and live! Our fathers disciplined us for a little while as they thought best; but God disciplines us for our good, that we may share in his holiness.

Hebrews 12:9–10

When we were children, we were in slavery under the basic principles of the world. But when the time had fully come, God sent his Son, born of a woman, born under law, to redeem those under law, that we might receive the full rights of sons. Because you are sons, God sent the Spirit of his Son into our hearts, the Spirit who calls out, "Abba, Father." So you are no longer a slave, but a son; and since you are a son, God has made you also an heir.

Galatians 4:3–7

GOD'S WORDS OF LIFE ON

FAMILY

As we have opportunity, let us do good to all people, especially to those who belong to the family of believers.

Galatians 6:10

I kneel before the Father, from whom his whole family in heaven and on earth derives its name.

Ephesians 3:14–15

If you belong to Christ, then you are Abraham's seed, and heirs according to the promise.

Galatians 3:29

The body is a unit, though it is made up of many parts; and though all its parts are many, they form one body. So it is with Christ. For we were all baptized by one Spirit into one body . . . and we were all given the one Spirit to drink.

1 Corinthians 12:12–13

FAMILY

Joseph set his eleven brothers against him by telling his dream of their bowing down to him. He was his father's favorite and perhaps he flaunted it. So when his brothers got a chance, they paid him back, selling him as a slave to Egypt.

In Egypt God brought Joseph to prominence in the land. But success was not enough. God wanted forgiveness within the family. When the brothers came to Egypt for help during a famine, Joseph felt the strain of forgiveness. He wanted to reconcile with his brothers, whom he loved, but it was not easy. But the story has a good ending—reconciliation finally occurred among the entire family.

Joseph's story points toward Jesus—a man God sent to save his people, one who was hated and betrayed by them just as Joseph was. But God's will to save conquers all. As Joseph told his brothers, "You intended to harm me, but God intended it for good to accomplish . . . the saving of many lives" (Genesis 50:20).

FORGIVENESS

If we confess our sins, God is faithful and just and will forgive us our sins and purify us from all unrighteousness.

1 John 1:9

God has rescued us from the dominion of darkness and brought us into the kingdom of the Son he loves, in whom we have redemption, the forgiveness of sins.

Colossians 1:13–14

Who is a God like you,
  who pardons sin and forgives the transgression
  of the remnant of his inheritance?
You do not stay angry forever
  but delight to show mercy.

Micah 7:18

Rend your heart
  and not your garments.
Return to the LORD your God,
  for he is gracious and compassionate,
slow to anger and abounding in love,
  and he relents from sending calamity.

Joel 2:13

The Lord our God is merciful and forgiving.

Daniel 9:9

FORGIVENESS

Be kind and compassionate to one another, forgiving each other, just as in Christ God forgave you.

Ephesians 4:32

God has reconciled you by Christ's physical body through death to present you holy in his sight, without blemish and free from accusation.

Colossians 1:22

You were washed, you were sanctified, you were justified in the name of the Lord Jesus Christ and by the Spirit of our God.

1 Corinthians 6:11

All the prophets testify about Jesus that everyone who believes in him receives forgiveness of sins through his name.

Acts 10:43

When you stand praying, if you hold anything against anyone, forgive him, so that your Father in heaven may forgive you your sins.

Mark 11:25

You forgave the iniquity of your people, O LORD, *and covered all their sins.*

Psalm 85:2

FORGIVENESS

Love your enemies, do good to them, and lend to them without expecting to get anything back. Then your reward will be great, and you will be sons of the Most High. . . . Be merciful, just as your Father is merciful.

Luke 6:35–36

God predestined us to be adopted as his sons through Jesus Christ, in accordance with his pleasure and will—to the praise of his glorious grace, which he has freely given us in the One he loves. In him we have redemption through his blood, the forgiveness of sins, in accordance with the riches of God's grace that he lavished on us with all wisdom and understanding.

Ephesians 1:5–8

As far as the east is from the west,
  so far has God removed our transgressions from us.

Psalm 103:12

Blessed is he
  whose transgressions are forgiven,
  whose sins are covered.

Psalm 32:1

FORGIVENESS

J esus told his followers, "Love your enemies and pray for those who persecute you" (Matthew 5:44). While everyone talks admiringly about that command, loving your enemies is no easy thing. Many people doubt whether it is even right. Should we forgive the Nazis? Should we make a point to be kind to the Ku Klux Klan?

The book of Jonah tells the story of a man whom God instructed to love his enemies in Nineveh. Jonah did just the opposite. He refused to go to the people he hated and tried to run away from the Lord.

Even though Jonah hated the people of Nineveh, God loved them. He wanted to save the city, not destroy it. When Jonah finally preached there, the entire city believed his message and repented. And the Lord forgave them.

Jonah needed to develop an attitude like God's toward his enemies. Insistently God led Jonah to this understanding of his own mind and heart. The book of Jonah is a story of a miraculous change in Nineveh, but even more a story of miraculous change in Jonah.

FRIENDS

Jesus said, "Love each other as I have loved you. Greater love has no one than this, that he lay down his life for his friends."

John 15:12–13

I am a friend to all who fear you, O LORD,
  to all who follow your precepts.

Psalm 119:63

There is a friend who sticks closer than a brother.

Proverbs 18:24

Jesus said, "I no longer call you servants, because a servant does not know his master's business. Instead, I have called you friends, for everything that I learned from my Father I have made known to you."

John 15:15

Jonathan said to David, "Go in peace, for we have sworn friendship with each other in the name of the LORD, saying, 'The LORD is witness between you and me, and between your descendants and my descendants forever.'"

1 Samuel 20:42

FRIENDS

The LORD would speak to Moses face to face, as a man speaks with his friend.

Exodus 33:11

My intercessor is my friend
as my eyes pour out tears to God;
on behalf of a man he pleads with God
as a man pleads for his friend.

Job 16:20–21

Perfume and incense bring joy to the heart,
and the pleasantness of one's friend springs
from his earnest counsel.

Proverbs 27:9

Two are better than one,
because they have a good return for their work:
If one falls down,
his friend can help him up.

Ecclesiastes 4:9–10

He who loves a pure heart and whose speech is gracious
will have the king for his friend.

Proverbs 22:11

FRIENDS

The scripture was fulfilled that says, "Abraham believed God, and it was credited to him as righteousness," and he was called God's friend.

James 2:23

Though one may be overpowered,
two can defend themselves.
A cord of three strands is not quickly broken.

Ecclesiastes 4:12

Let us not give up meeting together, as some are in the habit of doing, but let us encourage one another.

Hebrews 10:25

Glorify the LORD *with me;*
let us exalt his name together.

Psalm 34:3

A friend loves at all times.

Proverbs 17:17

FRIENDS

Jonathan faced a loyalty dilemma with his father, who grew insanely jealous of his son's friendship with David.

Though Jonathan had tried to stay loyal to both father and friend, his father made it impossible. Soon Jonathan realized that Saul would kill David if he caught him.

One major factor further complicated Jonathan's choice: As Saul's son, he stood next in line for the throne. By siding with David, he would ultimately harm himself. Even so, at the risk of his own neck, Jonathan chose to help David escape. He told David he would happily follow his friend as his number-two man (1 Samuel 23:17).

Tragically, the two friends never got the chance to rule together. In a battle against the Philistines, Jonathan fought at his father's side and was killed (1 Samuel 31:2). David, mourning his dearest friend, sang a poignant song in tribute (2 Samuel 1:17–27). Their loyalty and love make for one of the most beautiful stories of friendship ever told.

FUTURE PLANS

Trust in the LORD with all your heart
and lean not on your own understanding;
in all your ways acknowledge him,
and he will make your paths straight.

Proverbs 3:5–6

"I know the plans I have for you," declares the
LORD, "plans to prosper you and not to harm
you, plans to give you hope and a future."

Jeremiah 29:11

If the LORD delights in a man's way,
he makes his steps firm.

Psalm 37:23

Whether you turn to the right or to the left,
your ears will hear a voice behind you, saying,
"This is the way; walk in it."

Isaiah 30:21

Commit your way to the LORD;
trust in him and he will do this:
He will make your righteousness shine like the dawn,
the justice of your cause like the noonday sun.

Psalm 37:5–6

FUTURE PLANS

In his heart a man plans his course,
  but the LORD determines his steps.

Proverbs 16:9

Delight yourself in the LORD
  and he will give you the desires of your heart.

Psalm 37:4

Who, then, is the man that fears the LORD?
He will instruct him in the way chosen for him.

Psalm 25:12

Do not let this Book of the Law depart from
your mouth; meditate on it day and night,
so that you may be careful to do everything
written in it. Then you will be prosperous and
successful.

Joshua 1:8

God who began a good work in you will carry it
on to completion until the day of Christ Jesus.

Philippians 1:6

FUTURE PLANS

Consider the blameless, observe the upright;
   there is a future for the man of peace.

Psalm 37:37

Wisdom is sweet to your soul;
   if you find it, there is a future hope for you,
   and your hope will not be cut off.

Proverbs 24:14

May the LORD give you the desire of your heart
   and make all your plans succeed.

Psalm 20:4

Commit to the LORD whatever you do,
   and your plans will succeed.

Proverbs 16:3

When he, the Spirit of truth, comes, he will
guide you into all truth. He will not speak
on his own; he will speak only what he hears,
and he will tell you what is yet to come.

John 16:13

FUTURE PLANS

Be strong and courageous. Do not be terrified; do not be discouraged, for the LORD your God will be with you wherever you go.

Joshua 1:9

"I *will instruct you and teach you in the*
   way you should go;
I *will counsel you and watch over you,"*
   says the LORD.

Psalm 32:8

I am convinced that neither death nor life, neither angels nor demons, neither the present nor the future, nor any powers, neither height nor depth, nor anything else in all creation, will be able to separate us from the love of God that is in Christ Jesus our Lord.

Romans 8:38–39

FUTURE PLANS

It is God who makes ... you stand firm in Christ. He anointed us, set his seal of ownership on us, and put his Spirit in our hearts as a deposit, guaranteeing what is to come.

2 Corinthians 1:21–22

"I make known the end from the beginning,
  from ancient times, what is still to come,"
declares the LORD.

Isaiah 46:10

Forgetting what is behind and straining toward what is ahead, I press on toward the goal to win the prize for which God has called me heavenward in Christ Jesus.

Philippians 3:13–14

FUTURE PLANS

G od is in control—a message vividly portrayed to Jeremiah as he watched a potter start over on a pot that did not take the shape he wanted it to take. Israelites had gradually come to think that God, because he had chosen them as his people, was obliged to protect them. But their ungrateful behavior toward him had brought God to the point of "starting over" with them. In Romans 9:21, Paul returned to this metaphor to answer people who were claiming God was unjust.

In your future plans, remember to first consult God—he is forming your life for your good and his glory.

GOD'S GRACE

Praise be to the God and Father of our Lord Jesus Christ, who has blessed us in the heavenly realms with every spiritual blessing in Christ. For he chose us in him before the creation of the world to be holy and blameless in his sight. In love he predestined us to be adopted as his sons through Jesus Christ, in accordance with his pleasure and will—to the praise of his glorious grace, which he has freely given us in the One he loves. In him we have redemption through his blood, the forgiveness of sins, in accordance with the riches of God's grace that he lavished on us with all wisdom and understanding.

Ephesians 1:3–8

Let us . . . approach the throne of grace with confidence, so that we may receive mercy and find grace to help us in our time of need.

Hebrews 4:16

From the fullness of God's grace we have all received one blessing after another.

John 1:16

GOD'S GRACE

A righteousness from God, apart from law, has been made known, to which the Law and the Prophets testify. This righteousness from God comes through faith in Jesus Christ to all who believe. There is no difference, for all have sinned and fall short of the glory of God, and are justified freely by his grace through the redemption that came by Christ Jesus.

Romans 3:21–24

I always thank God for you because of his grace given you in Christ Jesus.

1 Corinthians 1:4

By the grace of God I am what I am, and his grace to me was not without effect.

1 Corinthians 15:10

God raised us up with Christ and seated us with him in the heavenly realms in Christ Jesus, in order that in the coming ages he might show the incomparable riches of his grace, expressed in his kindness to us in Christ Jesus. For it is by grace you have been saved, through faith—and this not from yourselves, it is the gift of God.

Ephesians 2:6–8

GOD'S GRACE

God is able to make all grace abound to you,
so that in all things at all times, having all that
you need, you will abound in every good work.

2 Corinthians 9:8

When the kindness and love of God our Savior
appeared, he saved us, not because of righteous
things we had done, but because of his mercy.
He saved us through the washing of rebirth
and renewal by the Holy Spirit, whom he
poured out on us generously through Jesus
Christ our Savior, so that, having been justified
by his grace, we might become heirs having the
hope of eternal life.

Titus 3:4–7

To each one of us grace has been given as
Christ apportioned it.

Ephesians 4:7

GOD'S GRACE

Jacob had a dream in which he saw a
stairway resting on the earth, with its top
reaching to heaven, and the angels of
God were ascending and descending on it.

Genesis 28:12

God's grace: this is what Jacob found while
traveling alone in the desert. Through his
own greedy scheming he had won the family
birthright and then, ironically, he had to run
away from the family. Yet God came to him full
of promises, not the reproaches he deserved.
Jacob had not looked for God, but God looked
for him. Jacob's vision of a stairway to heaven
looked forward to Jesus, who himself is the
bridge between heaven and earth (John 1:51).

GOD'S WILL

Do not conform any longer to the pattern of this world, but be transformed by the renewing of your mind. Then you will be able to test and approve what God's will is—his good, pleasing and perfect will.

Romans 12:2

Be joyful always; pray continually; give thanks in all circumstances, for this is God's will for you in Christ Jesus.

1 Thessalonians 5:16–18

Our Father in heaven,
hallowed be your name,
your kingdom come,
your will be done
   on earth as it is in heaven.

Matthew 6:9–10

The world and its desires pass away, but the man who does the will of God lives forever.

1 John 2:17

It is God who works in you to will and to act according to his good purpose.

Philippians 2:13

Stand at the crossroads and look; ask for the ancient paths, ask where the good way is, and walk in it.

Jeremiah 6:16

Jesus prayed, "Father, if you are willing, take this cup from me; yet not my will, but yours be done."

Luke 22:42

The Lord is not slow in keeping his promise, as some understand slowness. He is patient with you, not wanting anyone to perish, but everyone to come to repentance.

2 Peter 3:9

Salvation, which was first announced by the Lord, was confirmed to us by those who heard him. God also testified to it by signs, wonders and various miracles, and gifts of the Holy Spirit distributed according to his will.

Hebrews 2:3–4

GOD'S WILL

God made known to us the mystery of his will according to his good pleasure, which he purposed in Christ, to be put into effect when the times will have reached their fulfillment— to bring all things in heaven and on earth together under one head, even Christ.

Ephesians 1:9–10

May the God of peace . . . equip you with every-thing good for doing his will, and may he work in us what is pleasing to him, through Jesus Christ, to whom be glory for ever and ever. Amen.

Hebrews 13:20–21

This is the confidence we have in approaching God: that if we ask anything according to his will, he hears us. And if we know that he hears us—whatever we ask—we know that we have what we asked of him.

1 John 5:14–15

GOD'S WILL

Dressed in Esau's clothes and some fresh goatskins, Jacob flatly lied to his father and took the Lord's name in vain. And he didn't noticeably improve his ways later in life. He certainly doesn't seem like choice material for a religious leader.

But God chose Jacob. He was always making those kinds of choices with no apparent reason at all. Often he went against the time-honored practice of letting the firstborn son be number one, as he did in choosing Abel, Jacob, and Ephraim. In fact, an inspired prophecy marked Jacob as God's choice before he was even born —before he had done a single thing to merit the choice.

So God's choice did not necessarily depend on how a person behaved. God chose the one he wanted—it was as simple as that.

Is that fair? That's what the apostle Paul asked in Romans 9. He concluded that we have no right to find fault with God's choices, knowing as little as we do compared with his infinite understanding. Unquestionably, those choices worked for good—and the whole world became eligible to join the "chosen people." (See Galatians 3:26–29.)

GROWTH

Like newborn babies, crave pure spiritual milk,
so that by it you may grow up in your salvation,
now that you have tasted that the Lord is good.

1 Peter 2:2–3

My son, keep your father's commands
and do not forsake your mother's teaching. . . .
When you walk, they will guide you;
when you sleep, they will watch over you;
when you awake, they will speak to you.
For these commands are a lamp,
this teaching is a light,
and the corrections of discipline
are the way to life.

Proverbs 6:20, 22–23

When he, the Spirit of truth, comes, he will
guide you into all truth.

John 16:13

We, who with unveiled faces all reflect the
Lord's glory, are being transformed into his
likeness with ever-increasing glory, which
comes from the Lord, who is the Spirit.

2 Corinthians 3:18

Since the day we heard about you, we have not stopped praying for you and asking God to fill you with the knowledge of his will through all spiritual wisdom and understanding. And we pray this in order that you may live a life worthy of the Lord and may please him in every way: bearing fruit in every good work, growing in the knowledge of God, being strengthened with all power according to his glorious might so that you may have great endurance and patience, and joyfully giving thanks to the Father, who has qualified you to share in the inheritance of the saints in the kingdom of light.

Colossians 1:9–12

God's divine power has given us everything we need for life and godliness through our knowledge of him who called us by his own glory and goodness. . . . For this very reason, make every effort to add to your faith goodness; and to goodness, knowledge; and to knowledge, self-control; and to self-control, perseverance; and to perseverance, godliness; and to godliness, brotherly kindness; and to brotherly kindness, love.

2 Peter 1:3, 5–7

GROWTH

God who began a good work in you will carry it on to completion until the day of Christ Jesus.

Philippians 1:6

I pray that out of God's glorious riches he may strengthen you with power through his Spirit in your inner being, so that Christ may dwell in your hearts through faith. And I pray that you, being rooted and established in love, may have power, together with all the saints, to grasp how wide and long and high and deep is the love of Christ, and to know this love that surpasses knowledge—that you may be filled to the measure of all the fullness of God.

Ephesians 3:16–19

The righteous will flourish like a palm tree,
they will grow like a cedar of Lebanon;
planted in the house of the LORD,
they will flourish in the courts of our God.
They will still bear fruit in old age,
they will stay fresh and green.

Psalm 92:12–14

Whoever lives by the truth comes into the light, so that it may be seen plainly that what he has done has been done through God.

John 3:21

GROWTH

Bookstores are full of "how-to" books, each promising to teach you how to make a success of yourself by just following a few simple rules. Is Proverbs an ancient "how-to" book? It seems, at first look, more interested in success and prosperity than in God. Many of the proverbs can be adopted by those who have no love for God.

But if you look at Proverbs as a book, rather than a collection of unrelated fragments, you will find that its "how-tos" of wise living can't be separated from God. While some proverbs observe the hard facts of life—that bribes are effective, for instance, or that money does buy friends of a kind—the book never for a moment endorses success techniques that involve immorality. More important, a deep sense of people's sin and their utter dependence on God pervades proverbs. Wisdom, that fundamental tool for living, starts with the fear of God and leads to a knowledge of him.

GUIDANCE

"I will instruct you and teach you
   in the way you should go;
I will counsel you and watch over you,"
   says the LORD.

Psalm 32:8

You guide me with your counsel, O LORD,
   and afterward you will take me into glory.

Psalm 73:24

Plans fail for lack of counsel,
   but with many advisers they succeed.

Proverbs 15:22

The LORD will guide you always;
   he will satisfy your needs in a sun-scorched land
   and will strengthen your frame.
You will be like a well-watered garden,
   like a spring whose waters never fail.

Isaiah 58:11

Your word is a lamp to my feet
   and a light for my path, O LORD.

Psalm 119:105

GUIDANCE

Show me your ways, O LORD,
  teach me your paths;
guide me in your truth and teach me,
  for you are God my Savior,
  and my hope is in you all day long.

Psalm 25:4–5

Since you are my rock and my fortress, O LORD,
  for the sake of your name lead and guide me.

Psalm 31:3

Send forth your light and your truth, O God,
  let them guide me;
let them bring me to your holy mountain,
  to the place where you dwell.

Psalm 43:3

If I go up to the heavens, you are there, O LORD;
  if I make my bed in the depths, you are there.
If I rise on the wings of the dawn,
  if I settle on the far side of the sea,
even there your hand will guide me,
  your right hand will hold me fast.

Psalm 139:8–10

GUIDANCE

The LORD makes me lie down in green pastures,
    he leads me beside quiet waters,
    he restores my soul.
He guides me in paths of righteousness
    for his name's sake.

Psalm 23:2–3

Teach me to do your will,
    for you are my God;
may your good Spirit
    lead me on level ground.

Psalm 143:10

"I will give you shepherds after my own heart,
who will lead you with knowledge and understanding," says the LORD.

Jeremiah 3:15

For lack of guidance a nation falls,
    but many advisers make victory sure.

Proverbs 11:14

Make plans by seeking advice.

Proverbs 20:18

GUIDANCE

T hough the angel of the Lord had assured Gideon of success in battle, he took fright and wanted to double-check, then triple-check, by asking for miracles involving a wool fleece.

In contrast, the story of Ruth shows how God guides us even when we are not aware of it. Behind Ruth's eloquent story looms an invisible helper—God. He didn't intervene in the events, so far as the story tells. But nobody in Ruth doubted that life proceeded under God's direction. It was the Lord by whom Ruth swore when declaring her love to Naomi (Ruth 1:17), and the Lord whom Naomi credited for bringing Ruth to Boaz's field (2:20). God's law brought Boaz and Ruth into marriage. Finally, the Lord gave them a son, in whom the whole family found deep satisfaction.

The last verses of Ruth further show that God's plan extended beyond Ruth and Naomi —he was accepting a Moabite woman into his family. God's guidance in Ruth's life revealed a major truth, that his love was even for those outside of Israel.

It's comforting to know that God guides you through life, no matter what. He is always leading you as you live for him.

HEAVEN

Jesus said, "In my Father's house are many rooms; if it were not so, I would have told you. I am going there to prepare a place for you. And if I go and prepare a place for you, I will come back and take you to be with me that you also may be where I am."

John 14:2–3

Before me was a great multitude that no one could count. . . .
They are before the throne of God
  and serve him day and night in his temple;
and he who sits on the throne will spread his
    tent over them.
Never again will they hunger;
  never again will they thirst.
The sun will not beat upon them,
  nor any scorching heat.
For the Lamb at the center of the throne will
      be their shepherd;
  he will lead them to springs of living water.
And God will wipe away every tear from their eyes.

Revelation 7:9, 15–17

HEAVEN

There is in store for me the crown of righteousness, which the Lord, the righteous Judge, will award to me on that day—and not only to me, but also to all who have longed for his appearing.

2 Timothy 4:8

In keeping with God's promise we are looking forward to a new heaven and a new earth, the home of righteousness.

2 Peter 3:13

We will be with the Lord forever.

1 Thessalonians 4:17

The King will say to those on his right, "Come, you who are blessed by my Father; take your inheritance, the kingdom prepared for you since the creation of the world."

Matthew 25:34

Praise be to the God and Father of our Lord Jesus Christ! In his great mercy he has given us new birth into a living hope through the resurrection of Jesus Christ from the dead, and into an inheritance that can never perish, spoil or fade—kept in heaven for you.

1 Peter 1:3–4

HEAVEN

No eye has seen,
no ear has heard,
no mind has conceived
what God has prepared for those who love him.

1 Corinthians 2:9

I looked and there before me was a great multitude that no one could count, from every nation, tribe, people and language, standing before the throne and in front of the Lamb. They were wearing white robes and were holding palm branches in their hands. And they cried out in a loud voice:

"Salvation belongs to our God,
who sits on the throne,
and to the Lamb."

Revelation 7:9–10

Blessed are those who are persecuted because
of righteousness,
for theirs is the kingdom of heaven. . . .

Rejoice and be glad, because great is your reward in heaven.

Matthew 5:10, 12

HEAVEN

Jesus said, "To him who overcomes, I will give the right to sit with me on my throne, just as I overcame and sat down with my Father on his throne."

Revelation 3:21

In my vision at night I looked, and there before me was one like a son of man, coming with the clouds of heaven. He approached the Ancient of Days and was led into his presence. He was given authority, glory and sovereign power; all peoples, nations and men of every language worshiped him. His dominion is an everlasting dominion that will not pass away, and his kingdom is one that will never be destroyed.

Daniel 7:13–14

Jesus said, "The kingdom of heaven is like treasure hidden in a field. When a man found it, he hid it again, and then in his joy went and sold all he had and bought that field. Again, the kingdom of heaven is like a merchant looking for fine pearls. When he found one of great value, he went away and sold everything he had and bought it."

Matthew 13:44–46

81

HEAVEN

When Christ, who is your life, appears, then you also will appear with him in glory.

Colossians 3:4

Our citizenship is in heaven. And we eagerly await a Savior from there, the Lord Jesus Christ.

Philippians 3:20

There before me was a throne in heaven with someone sitting on it. And the one who sat there had the appearance of jasper and carnelian. A rainbow, resembling an emerald, encircled the throne. Surrounding the throne were twenty-four other thrones, and seated on them were twenty-four elders. They were dressed in white and had crowns of gold on their heads. From the throne came flashes of lightning, rumblings and peals of thunder. Before the throne, seven lamps were blazing. These are the seven spirits of God. Also before the throne there was what looked like a sea of glass, clear as crystal.

Revelation 4:2–6

HEAVEN

This world may be full of pollution, war, crime, and hate. But inside us linger dreams of what the world could be like. The Old Testament prophets dreamed of "that day" when creation would be made new. And those sensations, following a dismal monotone of predicted catastrophes, burst out of the last few chapters of Revelation. That perfect world is not merely a dream; it will come true.

There will be no more tears then, nor pain. Wild animals will frolic, not kill. Once again creation will work the way God intended. Peace will reign not only between God and individuals but between him and all creation. The kingdom comes out into the open. The City of God flings wide its gates.

Revelation ends on a note of great triumph. Somehow, out of all the bad news [foretold] here, good news emerges—spectacular Good News. To those who believe, Revelation becomes a book not of fear but of hope. God will prevail. All will be made new. It ends with a reunion—a marriage, Revelation calls it. There is a happy ending after all.

HOPE

Find rest, O my soul, in God alone;
    my hope comes from him.

Psalm 62:5

No one whose hope is in you, LORD,
    will ever be put to shame.

Psalm 25:3

Guide me in your truth and teach me,
    for you are God my Savior,
    and my hope is in you all day long.

Psalm 25:5

May integrity and uprightness protect me,
    because my hope is in you, O LORD.

Psalm 25:21

The eyes of the LORD are on those who fear him,
    on those whose hope is in his unfailing love.

Psalm 33:18

The LORD is good to those whose hope is in him,
    to the one who seeks him.

Lamentations 3:25

Blessed is he whose help is the God of Jacob,
  whose hope is in the LORD his God,
the Maker of heaven and earth,
  the sea, and everything in them—
  the LORD, who remains faithful forever.

Psalm 146:5–6

Do any of the worthless idols of the nations bring rain?
  Do the skies themselves send down showers?
No, it is you, O LORD our God.
  Therefore our hope is in you,
  for you are the one who does all this.

Jeremiah 14:22

This I call to mind ✓
  and therefore I have hope:
Because of the LORD's great love we are not consumed,
  for his compassions never fail.

Lamentations 3:21–22

You have been my hope, O Sovereign LORD, ✓
  my confidence since my youth.

Psalm 71:5

HOPE

Everything that was written in the past was written to teach us, so that through endurance and the encouragement of the Scriptures we might have hope.

Romans 15:4

I *watch in hope for the* LORD,
    I *wait for God my Savior;*
    my God will hear me.

Micah 7:7

Dear friends, now we are children of God, and what we will be has not yet been made known. But we know that when Christ appears, we shall be like him, for we shall see him as he is. Everyone who has this hope in him purifies himself, just as he is pure.

1 John 3:2–3

Through Christ you believe in God, who raised him from the dead and glorified him, and so your faith and hope are in God.

1 Peter 1:21

We always thank God, the Father of our Lord
Jesus Christ, when we pray for you, because
we have heard of your faith in Christ Jesus and
of the love you have for all the saints— the
faith and love that spring from the hope that
is stored up for you in heaven and that you
have already heard about in the word of truth,
the gospel.

Colossians 1:3–5

Praise be to the God and Father of our Lord
Jesus Christ! In his great mercy he has given
us new birth into a living hope through the
resurrection of Jesus Christ from the dead.

1 *Peter* 1:3

God wanted to make the unchanging nature of
his purpose very clear to the heirs of what was
promised, he confirmed it with an oath. God
did this so that, by two unchangeable things
in which it is impossible for God to lie, we who
have fled to take hold of the hope offered to us
may be greatly encouraged. We have this hope
as an anchor for the soul, firm and secure.

Hebrews 6:17–19

HOPE

Let us hold unswervingly to the hope we profess, for God who promised is faithful.

Hebrews 10:23

Set your hope fully on the grace to be given you when Jesus Christ is revealed.

1 Peter 1:13

When the kindness and love of God our Savior appeared, he saved us, not because of righteous things we had done, but because of his mercy. He saved us through the washing of rebirth and renewal by the Holy Spirit, whom he poured out on us generously through Jesus Christ our Savior, so that, having been justified by his grace, we might become heirs having the hope of eternal life.

Titus 3:4–7

HOPE

Isaiah 40–66 breaks into a majestic message of hope and joy and light. The prophet sets out to reestablish faith in God. He tells how God had in mind a new thing, a plan far more grand than anything seen before.

The author of Isaiah expresses the plan as a series of wonderful reasons for hope. First, he says, will come deliverance from the Babylonian captivity. A new star, a ruler named Cyrus, will arise in the east and set the Jews free. He will allow them to return to Jerusalem to begin the long task of rebuilding a city and a nation.

In words that have become very familiar, the book of Isaiah tells of two further hopes for the future. A mysterious figure called "the servant" appears in chapter 49. That servant, through his suffering, will provide a way to rescue the entire world. In conclusion, the prophet turns to a faraway time, when God will usher in peace for all in a new heaven and new earth. "The Holy One of Israel" will rule as the God of the whole earth.

IDENTITY

I *praise you, O* LORD, *because I am fearfully and
wonderfully made;
your works are wonderful,
I know that full well.*

Psalm 139:14

As a bridegroom rejoices over his bride,
so will your God rejoice over you.

Isaiah 62:5

The LORD your God is with you,
he is mighty to save.
He will take great delight in you,
he will quiet you with his love,
he will rejoice over you with singing.

Zephaniah 3:17

You brought me out of the womb, O LORD;
you made me trust in you
even at my mother's breast.
From birth I was cast upon you;
from my mother's womb you have been my God.

Psalm 22:9–10

IDENTITY

To all who received Christ, to those who believed in his name, he gave the right to become children of God.

John 1:12

My frame was not hidden from you, O LORD,
when I was made in the secret place.
When I was woven together in the depths of the earth,
your eyes saw my unformed body.
All the days ordained for me
were written in your book
before one of them came to be.

Psalm 139:15–16

Those who are led by the Spirit of God are sons of God. For you did not receive a spirit that makes you a slave again to fear, but you received the Spirit of sonship. And by him we cry, "Abba, Father." The Spirit himself testifies with our spirit that we are God's children. Now if we are children, then we are heirs— heirs of God and co-heirs with Christ, if indeed we share in his sufferings in order that we may also share in his glory.

Romans 8:14–17

IDENTITY

How great is the love the Father has lavished on us, that we should be called children of God! And that is what we are!

1 John 3:1

If anyone is in Christ, he is a new creation; the old has gone, the new has come!

2 Corinthians 5:17

God made Christ who had no sin to be sin for us, so that in him we might become the righteousness of God.

2 Corinthians 5:21

You are all sons of God through faith in Christ Jesus, for all of you who were baptized into Christ have clothed yourselves with Christ. There is neither Jew nor Greek, slave nor free, male nor female, for you are all one in Christ Jesus. If you belong to Christ, then you are Abraham's seed, and heirs according to the promise.

Galatians 3:26–29

"Before I formed you in the womb I knew you,
before you were born I set you apart,"
says the LORD.

Jeremiah 1:5

Jesus said, "Whoever does God's will is my brother and sister and mother."

Mark 3:35

You are a chosen people, a royal priesthood, a holy nation, a people belonging to God, that you may declare the praises of him who called you out of darkness into his wonderful light. Once you were not a people, but now you are the people of God; once you had not received mercy, but now you have received mercy.

1 *Peter* 2:9–10

Don't let anyone look down on you because you are young, but set an example for the believers in speech, in life, in love, in faith and in purity.

1 *Timothy* 4:12

You are all sons of the light and sons of the day.

1 *Thessalonians* 5:5

IDENTITY

You were once darkness, but now you are light in the Lord. Live as children of light (for the fruit of the light consists in all goodness, righteousness and truth) and find out what pleases the Lord.

Ephesians 5:8–10

You are no longer foreigners and aliens, but fellow citizens with God's people and members of God's household, built on the foundation of the apostles and prophets, with Christ Jesus himself as the chief cornerstone. In him the whole building is joined together and rises to become a holy temple in the Lord. And in him you too are being built together to become a dwelling in which God lives by his Spirit.

Ephesians 2:19–22

IDENTITY

When God describes the depth of his feelings for his people and tells us who we are in Christ, he uses tender language, as a parent with child. Psalm 139 is a good example of how much the Lord thinks of his people.

Does life begin at conception or at birth? Psalm 139 doesn't directly answer that question, but it does make clear that God's loving involvement with our lives starts long before birth. Nothing can escape God's concern, according to this psalm—no person, no thought, no place, and no time.

We cannot escape the fact that God cares for us deeply as a parent does for his or her child. How wonderful for us to "hear" his thoughts for his people through Scripture.

JOY

You will go out in joy
  and be led forth in peace;
the mountains and hills
  will burst into song before you,
and all the trees of the field
  will clap their hands.

Isaiah 55:12

Those who sow in tears
  will reap with songs of joy.
He who goes out weeping,
  carrying seed to sow,
will return with songs of joy,
  carrying sheaves with him.

Psalm 126:5–6

Light is shed upon the righteous
  and joy on the upright in heart.
Rejoice in the LORD, you who are righteous,
  and praise his holy name.

Psalm 97:11–12

Shouts of joy and victory
　　resound in the tents of the righteous:
"The LORD's right hand has done mighty things!"

Psalm 118:15

Jesus said, "As the Father has loved me, so
have I loved you. Now remain in my love. . . .
I have told you this so that my joy may be in
you and that your joy may be complete."

John 15:9, 11

I will rejoice in the LORD,
　　I will be joyful in God my Savior.

Habakkuk 3:18

The ransomed of the LORD will return.
　　They will enter Zion with singing;
　　everlasting joy will crown their heads.
Gladness and joy will overtake them,
　　and sorrow and sighing will flee away.

Isaiah 51:11

Though you have not seen Jesus, you love him;
and even though you do not see him now, you
believe in him and are filled with an inexpressible
and glorious joy.

1 Peter 1:8

JOY

The joy of the LORD is your strength.

Nehemiah 8:10

I *delight greatly in the* LORD;
my soul rejoices in my God.
For *he has clothed me with garments of salvation*
and arrayed me in a robe of righteousness,
as a bridegroom adorns his head like a priest,
and as a bride adorns herself with her jewels.

Isaiah 61:10

Jesus said, "I will see you again and you will
rejoice, and no one will take away your joy."

John 16:22

Let *all who take refuge in you be glad;*
let them ever sing for joy.
Spread your protection over them,
that those who love your name may rejoice in you.
For *surely, O* LORD, *you bless the righteous;*
you surround them with your favor as with a shield.

Psalm 5:11–12

Clap your hands, all you nations;
　shout to God with cries of joy.
How awesome is the LORD Most High,
　the great King over all the earth!

Psalm 47:1–2

Worship the LORD with gladness;
　come before him with joyful songs.

Psalm 100:2

Sing to God, sing praise to his name,
　extol him who rides on the clouds—
his name is the LORD—
　and rejoice before him.

Psalm 68:4

We rejoice in the hope of the glory of God.

Romans 5:2

We . . . rejoice in God through our Lord Jesus
Christ, through whom we have now received
reconciliation.

Romans 5:11

JOY

Let the heavens rejoice, let the earth be glad;
  let the sea resound, and all that is in it;
  let the fields be jubilant, and everything in them.
Then all the trees of the forest will sing for joy.

Psalm 96:11–12

This is the day the LORD has made;
  let us rejoice and be glad in it.

Psalm 118:24

Rejoice in the Lord always. I will say it again:
Rejoice!

Philippians 4:4

JOY

Rejoice in the Lord!

Philippians 3:1

Joy. The word has a quick, poignant ring to it. Yet it, like other words, has been drained of meaning over the years. Nowadays *joy* is used most commonly for a sensation like *thrill*. Paul had a different understanding of the word, as his letter to the Philippians reveals.

Philippians uses the word *joy* or *rejoice* every few paragraphs, but the joy it describes doesn't vanish after your heart starts beating normally again. Rejoice, says Paul, when someone selfishly tries to steal the limelight from you. And when you meet persecution for your faith. In fact, the most joyous book in the Bible comes from the pen of an author chained to a Roman guard. How could a rational man devote a letter to the topic of joy while his survival was in serious jeopardy?

Paul hints at an answer in a burst of eloquence in chapter 2 (verses 5–11). In it, Paul discusses Christ's perspective in coming to earth. The cross, and Jesus' resurrection, proves that nothing is powerful enough to stamp out a reason for joy—joy "in the Lord," as Paul says.

KNOWLEDGE

The *fear of the* LORD *is the beginning of knowledge.*

Proverbs 1:7

The *heavens declare the glory of God;*
the skies proclaim the work of his hands.
Day *after day they pour forth speech;*
night after night they display knowledge.

Psalm 19:1–2

My *son, if you accept my words*
and store up my commands within you,
turning your ear to wisdom
and applying your heart to understanding, . . .
then you will understand the fear of the LORD
and find the knowledge of God.
For *the* LORD *gives wisdom,*
and from his mouth come knowledge and
understanding. . . .
Wisdom *will enter your heart,*
and knowledge will be pleasant to your soul.

Proverbs 2:1–2, 5–6, 10

Teach *me knowledge and good judgment, O* LORD,
for I believe in your commands.

Psalm 119:66

KNOWLEDGE

The heart of the discerning acquires knowledge;
the ears of the wise seek it out.

Proverbs 18:15

My son, pay attention to my wisdom,
listen well to my words of insight,
that you may maintain discretion
and your lips may preserve knowledge.

Proverbs 5:1–2

This is my prayer: that your love may abound
more and more in knowledge and depth of
insight.

Philippians 1:9

Gold there is, and rubies in abundance,
but lips that speak knowledge are a rare jewel.

Proverbs 20:15

Thanks be to God, who always leads us in
triumphal procession in Christ and through
us spreads everywhere the fragrance of the
knowledge of him.

2 Corinthians 2:14

KNOWLEDGE

"I will give you shepherds after my own heart, who will lead you with knowledge and understanding," says the LORD.

Jeremiah 3:15

A wise man has great power,
and a man of knowledge increases strength.

Proverbs 24:5

Jesus said, "The knowledge of the secrets of the kingdom of God has been given to you."

Luke 8:10

To the man who pleases him, God gives wisdom, knowledge and happiness.

Ecclesiastes 2:26

God will be the sure foundation for your times,
a rich store of salvation and wisdom and knowledge;
the fear of the LORD is the key to this treasure.

Isaiah 33:6

KNOWLEDGE

The fear of the LORD *is the beginning of knowledge.*

Proverbs 1:7

T he phrase "the fear of the LORD" doesn't mean fright or terror. It means "a good relationship with God," based on reverence and respect for him and his commands. In Proverbs, for instance, the fear of the Lord means righteous living.

Although the fear of the Lord is the beginning of knowledge, human knowledge has an end—there is no match for God's infinite knowledge and understanding. In Ecclesiastes, even the Teacher, a man who possessed brilliant powers of knowledge and wisdom and observation, had to conclude that some things are beyond understanding. Failing in his attempt to "figure out" life, he fell back on simple advice: Fear God and obey him, no matter how things seem to you. In essence, he concluded in favor of a life of faith.

LONELINESS

God sets the lonely in families,
   he leads forth the prisoners with singing.

Psalm 68:6

God has said,
"Never will I leave you;
   never will I forsake you."

Hebrews 13:5

I am always with you, LORD;
   you hold me by my right hand.

Psalm 73:23

The LORD himself goes before you and will be
with you; he will never leave you nor forsake
you.

Deuteronomy 31:8

Jesus said, "Surely I am with you always, to the
very end of the age."

Matthew 28:20

Jesus said, "I will not leave you as orphans; I
will come to you."

John 14:18

LONELINESS

Jesus said, "I will ask the Father, and he will give you another Counselor to be with you forever—the Spirit of truth."

John 14:16–17

In Christ we who are many form one body, and each member belongs to all the others.

Romans 12:5

You are with me, LORD;
    your rod and your staff,
they comfort me.

Psalm 23:4

God said, "I am with you and will watch over you wherever you go. . . . I will not leave you until I have done what I have promised you."

Genesis 28:15

Those who know your name will trust in you,
    for you, LORD, have never forsaken those
who seek you.

Psalm 9:10

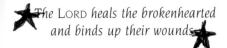

The LORD heals the brokenhearted
and binds up their wounds.

Psalm 147:3

Though my father and mother forsake me,
the LORD will receive me.

Psalm 27:10

Come near to God and he will come near to you.

James 4:8

LONELINESS

A t his last supper with his disciples, Jesus prepared his friends for his departure. Never before had Jesus been so direct with them. He fully recognized the significance of this last evening before his death.

"It is for your good that I am going away," Jesus said (John 16:7), but the disciples were too busy discussing the meaning of "going away" to comprehend the good that would follow. They thought only of how lonely they would be without him.

Nevertheless, Jesus kept explaining until at last the disciples showed signs of understanding. God's Son had entered the world to reside in one body. He was leaving earth to return to the Father. But he would not leave them lonely— the Spirit would come and reside in many bodies. Jesus knew that sending the Comforter to be with each of them at all times would be far better than his remaining with them.

What a comforting truth—now every believer has the Holy Spirit, God himself, living in them. He fulfilled his promise, "I will never leave you or forsake you" (Hebrews 13:5).

LOVE

This is how we know what love is: Jesus Christ laid down his life for us. And we ought to lay down our lives for our brothers.

1 John 3:16

Surely goodness and love will follow me
  all the days of my life,
and I will dwell in the house of the LORD
  forever.

Psalm 23:6

How great is the love the Father has lavished on us, that we should be called children of God!

1 John 3:1

May your unfailing love rest upon us, O LORD,
  even as we put our hope in you.

Psalm 33:22

Your love, O LORD, *reaches to the heavens,*
  your faithfulness to the skies.

Psalm 36:5

Love one another deeply, from the heart.

1 Peter 1:22

Love is patient, love is kind. It does not envy, it does not boast, it is not proud. It is not rude, it is not self-seeking, it is not easily angered, it keeps no record of wrongs. Love does not delight in evil but rejoices with the truth. It always protects, always trusts, always hopes, always perseveres. Love never fails.

1 Corinthians 13:4–8

I pray that you, being rooted and established in love, may have power, together with all the saints, to grasp how wide and long and high and deep is the love of Christ, and to know this love that surpasses knowledge—that you may be filled to the measure of all the fullness of God.

Ephesians 3:17–19

You are a forgiving God, gracious and compassionate, slow to anger and abounding in love.

Nehemiah 9:17

Jesus said, "If anyone loves me, he will obey my teaching. My Father will love him, and we will come to him and make our home with him."

John 14:23

111

LOVE

If you have any encouragement from being united with Christ, if any comfort from his love, if any fellowship with the Spirit, if any tenderness and compassion, then make my joy complete by being like-minded, having the same love, being one in spirit and purpose.

Philippians 2:1–2

I *love you*, O LORD, *my strength*.

Psalm 18:1

"*Though the mountains be shaken
    and the hills be removed,
yet my unfailing love for you will not be shaken
    nor my covenant of peace be removed*,"
    says the LORD, *who has compassion on you*.

Isaiah 54:10

I *trust in your unfailing love*, O LORD;
    my heart rejoices in your salvation.

Psalm 13:5

Because of the LORD's *great love we are not consumed,
    for his compassions never fail*.

Lamentations 3:22

LOVE

He who pursues righteousness and love
   finds life, prosperity and honor.

Proverbs 21:21

How priceless is your unfailing love, O LORD!
Both high and low among men
   find refuge in the shadow of your wings.

Psalm 36:7

Mercy, peace and love be yours in abundance.

Jude 2

Because your love is better than life, O LORD,
   my lips will glorify you.

Psalm 63:3

This is how God showed his love among us:
He sent his one and only Son into the world
that we might live through him. This is love:
not that we loved God, but that he loved us
and sent his Son as an atoning sacrifice for
our sins.

1 John 4:9–10

God is love. Whoever lives in love lives in God,
and God in him.

1 John 4:16

LOVE

I *will sing of the* LORD's *great love forever;*
   with my mouth I will make your faithfulness known
through all generations.

Psalm 89:1

As *high as the heavens are above the earth,*
   so great is God's love for those who fear him.

Psalm 103:11

Love the Lord your God with all your heart and
with all your soul and with all your strength
and with all your mind; and, love your neighbor
as yourself.

Luke 10:27

God has poured out his love into our hearts by
the Holy Spirit, whom he has given us.

Romans 5:5

May the Lord make your love increase and
overflow for each other.

1 Thessalonians 3:12

LOVE

Psalm 119 is a long, passionate love poem about God's law. How do you fall in love with the law? Most people admit that rules are necessary, and appreciate them grudgingly. But no one writes love poems to the federal drug statutes.

The word translated "law" doesn't merely mean rules. It expresses the totality of God's written instructions—his entire Word. The poet sees life full of uncertainties, and he understands that God has given a reliable guide for living—like pavement underfoot after you have been stuck in mud.

The psalmist simply does not see God's law as a dusty, rigid rule book. He hears God's loving voice in it. "The earth is filled with your love, O LORD; teach me your decrees" (verse 64).

God's laws channel God's love into the poet's life. They protect him from doing wrong and give him wisdom to understand his situation. They make new life flow into him. No wonder he writes with such thankfulness. In God's Word he finds more than direction. He finds love—God himself.

MONEY

The LORD is my shepherd, I shall not be in want.

Psalm 23:1

Fear the LORD, you his saints,
   for those who fear him lack nothing.
The lions may grow weak and hungry,
   but those who seek the LORD lack no good thing.

Psalm 34:9–10

Give, and it will be given to you. A good measure, pressed down, shaken together and running over, will be poured into your lap. For with the measure you use, it will be measured to you.

Luke 6:38

"Bring the whole tithe into the storehouse, that there may be food in my house. Test me in this," says the LORD Almighty, "and see if I will not throw open the floodgates of heaven and pour out so much blessing that you will not have room enough for it."

Malachi 3:10

A gift opens the way for the giver
   and ushers him into the presence of the great.

Proverbs 18:16

MONEY

When you give to the needy, do not let your left hand know what your right hand is doing, so that your giving may be in secret. Then your Father, who sees what is done in secret, will reward you.

Matthew 6:3–4

He who gathers money little by little makes it grow.

Proverbs 13:11

I was young and now I am old,
yet I have never seen the righteous forsaken
or their children begging bread.
They are always generous and lend freely;
their children will be blessed.

Psalm 37:25–26

Just as you excel in everything—in faith, in speech, in knowledge, in complete earnestness and in your love for us—see that you also excel in this grace of giving.

2 Corinthians 8:7

My God will meet all your needs according to his glorious riches in Christ Jesus.

Philippians 4:19

MONEY

The earth is the LORD's, and everything in it,
   the world, and all who live in it.

Psalm 24:1

Remember this: Whoever sows sparingly will also reap sparingly, and whoever sows generously will also reap generously. Each man should give what he has decided in his heart to give, not reluctantly or under compulsion, for God loves a cheerful giver. And God is able to make all grace abound to you, so that in all things at all times, having all that you need, you will abound in every good work.

2 Corinthians 9:6–8

Jesus said, "Love your enemies, do good to them, and lend to them without expecting to get anything back. Then your reward will be great, and you will be sons of the Most High."

Luke 6:35

Whoever trusts in his riches will fall, but the righteous will thrive like a green leaf.

Proverbs 11:28

"Poor people are lazy," one person says. Someone else claims the opposite: "They are poor because the rich control the system." People tend to oversimplify when they discuss wealth and poverty. Curiously, both sides may quote Proverbs to prove their point.

You may have to read all of Proverbs to get its subtle view. It says people are poor for various reasons: because of laziness and drunkenness, but also because the rich oppress them. People get rich for various reasons too: because of hard work, because of the Lord's blessing, because they cheated.

Proverbs gives an evenhanded view of what money does for people. Wealth brings benefits, including eager friends, Proverbs says, but it also brings worries and troubles. Proverbs strongly urges the rich and powerful to be generous and fair to poor people. It remains remarkably clear-eyed about the tangled causes of poverty and about the dangers and benefits of wealth.

PATIENCE

Be patient . . . until the Lord's coming. See how the farmer waits for the land to yield its valuable crop and how patient he is for the autumn and spring rains. You too, be patient and stand firm, because the Lord's coming is near.

James 5:7–8

Love is patient, love is kind.

1 Corinthians 13:4

A patient man has great understanding.

Proverbs 14:29

A *man's wisdom gives him patience;*
it is to his glory to overlook an offense.

Proverbs 19:11

It is good to wait quietly for the salvation of the LORD.

Lamentations 3:26

Be joyful in hope, patient in affliction, faithful in prayer.

Romans 12:12

A *hot-tempered man stirs up dissension,*
but a patient man calms a quarrel.

Proverbs 15:18

PATIENCE

I wait for the LORD, my soul waits,
   and in his word I put my hope.
My soul waits for the Lord
   more than watchmen wait for the morning.

Psalm 130:5–6

Jesus said, "Since you have kept my command to endure patiently, I will also keep you from the hour of trial that is going to come upon the whole world to test those who live on the earth."

Revelation 3:10

The Lord is not slow in keeping his promise, as some understand slowness. He is patient with you, not wanting anyone to perish, but everyone to come to repentance.

2 Peter 3:9

Better a patient man than a warrior,
   a man who controls his temper than
one who takes a city.

Proverbs 16:32

As God's chosen people, holy and dearly loved, clothe yourselves with compassion, kindness, humility, gentleness and patience.

Colossians 3:12

PATIENCE

Here is a trustworthy saying that deserves full acceptance: Christ Jesus came into the world to save sinners. . . . I was shown mercy so that in me, the worst of sinners, Christ Jesus might display his unlimited patience as an example for those who would believe on him and receive eternal life.

1 Timothy 1:15–16

There is a time for everything, and a season for every activity under heaven. . . . God has made everything beautiful in its time.

Ecclesiastes 3:1, 11

I *waited patiently for the* LORD;
he turned to me and heard my cry.

Psalm 40:1

*Since ancient times no one has heard,
no ear has perceived,
no eye has seen any God besides you,
who acts on behalf of those who wait for him.*

Isaiah 64:4

PATIENCE

How trusting and patient is a baby? Not very, some would say, for babies cry violently as soon as they feel the slightest hunger. It is the weaned child, a little older, who has learned to trust its mother, to fret less and simply ask for food instead of wailing. The profound simplicity of this patience is David's model for how he, and all God's people, should wait on the Lord. "I have stilled and quieted my soul; like a weaned child with its mother, like a weaned child is my soul within me" (Psalm 131:2). The apostle Paul comments similarly, "I have learned the secret of being content in any and every situation. . . . I can do everything through Christ who gives me strength" (Philippians 4:12–13). We think of needing to have patience with other people, but this teaches us to also have patience with God, because he will keep his promises to us if we wait patiently for him.

GOD'S WORDS OF LIFE ON
PEACE

The LORD *bless you*
   and keep you;
the LORD *make his face shine upon you*
   and be gracious to you;
the LORD *turn his face toward you*
   and give you peace.

Numbers 6:24–26

I *will lie down and sleep in peace,*
   for you alone, O LORD,
   make me dwell in safety.

Psalm 4:8

Jesus said, "In this world you will have trouble.
But take heart! I have overcome the world."

John 16:33

May the God of hope fill you with all joy
and peace as you trust in him, so that you
may overflow with hope by the power of the
Holy Spirit.

Romans 15:13

The LORD *gives strength to his people;*
   the LORD *blesses his people with peace.*

Psalm 29:11

PEACE

Wisdom's ways are pleasant ways,
and all her paths are peace.

Proverbs 3:17

Jesus said, "Peace I leave with you; my peace
I give you. I do not give to you as the world
gives. Do not let your hearts be troubled and
do not be afraid."

John 14:27

You will keep in perfect peace
him whose mind is steadfast,
because he trusts in you, O LORD.

Isaiah 26:3

Do not be anxious about anything, but
in everything, by prayer and petition, with
thanksgiving, present your requests to God.
The peace of God, which transcends all understanding, will guard your hearts and your
minds in Christ Jesus.

Philippians 4:6–7

A heart at peace gives life to the body.

Proverbs 14:30

PEACE

When a man's ways are pleasing to the LORD,
he makes even his enemies live at peace with him.

Proverbs 16:7

The fruit of the Spirit is love, joy, peace,
patience, kindness, goodness, faithfulness,
gentleness and self-control. Against such
things there is no law.

Galatians 5:22–23

Those who walk uprightly
enter into peace.

Isaiah 57:2

God said, "I will grant peace in the land,
and you will lie down and no one will make
you afraid."

Leviticus 26:6

You will go out in joy
and be led forth in peace.

Isaiah 55:12

Peacemakers who sow in peace raise a harvest
of righteousness.

James 3:18

PEACE

Let the peace of Christ rule in your hearts, since as members of one body you were called to peace.

Colossians 3:15

My people will live in peaceful dwelling places,
  in secure homes,
  in undisturbed places of rest.

Isaiah 32:18

May the Lord of peace himself give you peace at all times and in every way. The Lord be with all of you.

2 Thessalonians 3:16

Mercy, peace and love be yours in abundance.

Jude 2

Grace, mercy and peace from God the Father and from Jesus Christ, the Father's Son, will be with us in truth and love.

2 John 1:3

May the God of peace . . . equip you with everything good for doing his will.

Hebrews 13:20–21

127

PEACE

God is not a God of disorder but of peace.

1 Corinthians 14:33

Christ himself is our peace, who has made
the two one and has destroyed the barrier,
the dividing wall of hostility, by abolishing in
his flesh the law with its commandments and
regulations. His purpose was to create in himself one new man out of the two, thus making
peace, and in this one body to reconcile both
of them to God through the cross, by which
he put to death their hostility. He came and
preached peace to you who were far away and
peace to those who were near. For through
him we both have access to the Father by
one Spirit.

Ephesians 2:14–18

PEACE

I saiah looked at the world with a kind of split vision. Around him he saw spiritual decay and the dreary cycle of war and death. Yet God had given him a clear vision of what his nation could one day become: a pure people, faithful to God, living in peace with "war no more."

With God's view of the future shining brightly before him, Isaiah went about reinterpreting history. Others in Judah looked upon military invasions as terrible catastrophes. In contrast, Isaiah—though he felt anguish over the events —saw glimpses of a higher purpose.

The Jews were called by God to be a "light for the Gentiles," Isaiah said, a nation used by God to bring his truth to other nations. And out of the land of Judah God would raise up a great Prince of Peace who would rule over all the earth.

PERSEVERANCE

Since we are surrounded by such a great cloud of witnesses, let us throw off everything that hinders and the sin that so easily entangles, and let us run with perseverance the race marked out for us. Let us fix our eyes on Jesus, the author and perfecter of our faith, who for the joy set before him endured the cross, scorning its shame, and sat down at the right hand of the throne of God. Consider him who endured such opposition from sinful men, so that you will not grow weary and lose heart.

Hebrews 12:1–3

Do not throw away your confidence; it will be richly rewarded. You need to persevere so that when you have done the will of God, you will receive what he has promised.

Hebrews 10:35–36

We rejoice in the hope of the glory of God. Not only so, but we also rejoice in our sufferings, because we know that suffering produces perseverance; perseverance, character; and character, hope.

Romans 5:2–4

PERSEVERANCE

Let us not become weary in doing good, for at the proper time we will reap a harvest if we do not give up.

Galatians 6:9

Consider it pure joy, my brothers, whenever you face trials of many kinds, because you know that the testing of your faith develops perseverance. Perseverance must finish its work so that you may be mature and complete, not lacking anything.

James 1:2–4

Create in me a pure heart, O God,
and renew a steadfast spirit within me.

Psalm 51:10

We consider blessed those who have persevered. You have heard of Job's perseverance and have seen what the Lord finally brought about. The Lord is full of compassion and mercy.

James 5:11

PERSEVERANCE

The God of all grace, who called you to his eternal glory in Christ, after you have suffered a little while, will himself restore you and make you strong, firm and steadfast. To him be the power for ever and ever. Amen.

1 Peter 5:10–11

Make every effort to add to your faith goodness; and to goodness, knowledge; and to knowledge, self-control; and to self-control, perseverance; and to perseverance, godliness; and to godliness, brotherly kindness; and to brotherly kindness, love.

2 Peter 1:5–7

Jesus said, "I know your deeds, your hard work and your perseverance. . . . You have persevered and have endured hardships for my name, and have not grown weary."

Revelation 2:2–3

Jesus said, "In this world you will have trouble. But take heart! I have overcome the world."

John 16:33

PERSEVERANCE

> Train yourself to be godly. For physical training is of some value, but godliness has value for all things, holding promise for both the present life and the life to come.
>
> 1 Timothy 4:7–8

Paul uses the analogy of physical training in his letter to Timothy, urging him to train himself for godliness the same way disciplined athletes train for competition. Rather than physical barriers, Timothy faced personality barriers. Several times Paul refers to Timothy's reserved, timid disposition, which probably contributed to his chronic stomach trouble.

Given his shyness and his half-Jewish, half-Gentile ancestry, Timothy did not seem the ideal choice for a heresy fighter in a turbulent church. But Paul was convinced he could do the job. He encouraged Timothy with such motivational phrases as "I charge you" and "I urge you." He also reminded Timothy of his ordination, a commitment he had made long before.

Christians need a model, an example of how they should live, perhaps even more than they need words of wisdom. In First Timothy, Paul urges his loyal friend to become that model by accepting the discipline and hard work required.

PRAISE AND WORSHIP

Praise the LORD with the harp;
   make music to him on the ten-stringed lyre.
Sing to him a new song;
   play skillfully, and shout for joy.

Psalm 33:2–3

Ascribe to the LORD the glory due his name;
   worship the LORD in the splendor of his holiness.

Psalm 29:2

Jesus declared, "A time is coming and has now
come when the true worshipers will worship
the Father in spirit and truth, for they are
the kind of worshipers the Father seeks. God
is spirit, and his worshipers must worship in
spirit and in truth."

John 4:23–24

All the nations you have made
   will come and worship before you, O Lord;
   they will bring glory to your name.

Psalm 86:9

Is anyone happy? Let him sing songs of praise.

James 5:13

PRAISE AND WORSHIP

I heard every creature in heaven and on earth and under the earth and on the sea, and all that is in them, singing:

"To him who sits on the throne and to the Lamb be praise and honor and glory and power,
for ever and ever!"

Revelation 5:13

I will praise you with the harp
for your faithfulness, O my God;
I will sing praise to you with the lyre,
O Holy One of Israel.
My lips will shout for joy
when I sing praise to you—
I, whom you have redeemed.

Psalm 71:22–23

How good it is to sing praises to our God,
how pleasant and fitting to praise him!

Psalm 147:1

Let the word of Christ dwell in you richly as you teach and admonish one another with all wisdom, and as you sing psalms, hymns and spiritual songs with gratitude in your hearts to God.

Colossians 3:16

PRAISE AND WORSHIP

When Jesus came near the place where the road goes down the Mount of Olives, the whole crowd of disciples began joyfully to praise God in loud voices for all the miracles they had seen:

"Blessed is the king who comes in the name of the Lord!"
"Peace in heaven and glory in the highest!"

Luke 19:37–38

Sing to the LORD, sing praise to him;
   tell of all his wonderful acts.

1 Chronicles 16:9

All the earth bows down to you, O LORD;
   they sing praise to you,
   they sing praise to your name.

Psalm 66:4

Since we are receiving a kingdom that cannot be shaken, let us be thankful, and so worship God acceptably with reverence and awe.

Hebrews 12:28

PRAISE AND WORSHIP

Many of the psalms were meant to be sung, and sung joyfully. Modern church formality seems far removed from their frequent command: "Sing for joy! Shout aloud!" Their instruments included cymbals, tambourines, trumpets, ram's horns, harps, and lyres. Sometimes dancing erupted. The world, in the psalmist's imagination, can't contain the delight God inspires. A new song must be sung. "Shout for joy to the LORD, all the earth, burst into jubilant song" (Psalm 98:4).

First Chronicles 15:16 and 23:5 report that David appointed four thousand professional musicians to provide their services to the temple. They offered the best music available, and the congregation joined in. Nobody knows exactly what it sounded like, but scholars doubt it was all soft and soothing. Musicians improvised. Most of the instruments used suggest rousing, rhythmic sound.

Every generation of Christians renews the discovery of this "new song," sometimes through the music of their forbearers, sometimes in a form that shocks their solemn elders. When people know God, they come to life with a jubilant song on their lips.

PRAYER

Ask and it will be given to you; seek and you will find; knock and the door will be opened to you. For everyone who asks receives; he who seeks finds; and to him who knocks, the door will be opened.

Matthew 7:7–8

Jesus said, "I will do whatever you ask in my name, so that the Son may bring glory to the Father. You may ask me for anything in my name, and I will do it."

John 14:13–14

The prayer of a righteous man is powerful and effective.

James 5:16

When you pray, go into your room, close the door and pray to your Father, who is unseen. Then your Father, who sees what is done in secret, will reward you.

Matthew 6:6

Jesus said, "I tell you that if two of you on earth agree about anything you ask for, it will be done for you by my Father in heaven."

Matthew 18:19

Is any one of you sick? He should call the elders of the church to pray over him and anoint him with oil in the name of the Lord. And the prayer offered in faith will make the sick person well; the Lord will raise him up. If he has sinned, he will be forgiven.

James 5:14–15

If you believe, you will receive whatever you ask for in prayer.

Matthew 21:22

How gracious God will be when you cry for help! As soon as he hears, he will answer you.

Isaiah 30:19

The LORD *is near to all who call on him,*
 to all who call on him in truth.

Psalm 145:18

Do not be anxious about anything, but in everything, by prayer and petition, with thanksgiving, present your requests to God. And the peace of God, which transcends all understanding, will guard your hearts and your minds in Christ Jesus.

Philippians 4:6–7

PRAYER

This is the confidence we have in approaching God: that if we ask anything according to his will, he hears us. And if we know that he hears us—whatever we ask—we know that we have what we asked of him.

1 John 5:14–15

Jesus said, "If you remain in me and my words remain in you, ask whatever you wish, and it will be given you."

John 15:7

You will call, and the LORD will answer;
    you will cry for help, and he will say: Here am I.

Isaiah 58:9

Delight yourself in the LORD
    and he will give you the desires of your heart.

Psalm 37:4

"Call to me and I will answer you and tell you great and unsearchable things you do not know," declares the LORD.

Jeremiah 33:3

When I called, you answered me, LORD;
    you made me bold and stouthearted.

Psalm 138:3

"You will call upon me and come and pray to me, and I will listen to you. You will seek me and find me when you seek me with all your heart," says the LORD.

Jeremiah 29:12–13

The Spirit helps us in our weakness. We do not know what we ought to pray for, but the Spirit himself intercedes for us with groans that words cannot express. He who searches our hearts knows the mind of the Spirit, because the Spirit intercedes for the saints in accordance with God's will.

Romans 8:26–27

The eyes of the Lord are on the righteous
and his ears are attentive to their prayer.

1 *Peter* 3:12

I urge . . . that requests, prayers, intercession and thanksgiving be made for everyone—for kings and all those in authority, that we may live peaceful and quiet lives in all godliness and holiness. This is good, and pleases God our Savior, who wants all men to be saved and to come to a knowledge of the truth.

1 *Timothy* 2:1–4

PRAYER

"Before [my people] call I will answer;
   while they are still speaking I will hear,"
says the LORD.

Isaiah 65:24

Pray in the Spirit on all occasions with all
kinds of prayers and requests. With this in
mind, be alert and always keep on praying
for all the saints.

Ephesians 6:18

Jesus said, "This . . . is how you should pray:
'Our Father in heaven,
hallowed be your name,
your kingdom come,
your will be done
   on earth as it is in heaven.
Give us today our daily bread.
Forgive us our debts,
   as we also have forgiven our debtors.
And lead us not into temptation,
but deliver us from the evil one.'"

Matthew 6:9–13

PRAYER

Our prayers say a lot about who we are and how our relationship with God is going. For instance, Daniel's prayer in Daniel 2 gives insight into Daniel's spiritual life. It begins with expressing absolute confidence in God's control over the world: Daniel clung to such faith even while living in an enemy nation that had just destroyed God's temple in Jerusalem. Also, the prayer shows Daniel's spirit of humility and praise in the midst of crisis: he paused to give God credit before rushing to the king to interpret his dream.

Second Chronicles contains two great prayers: Solomon's in chapter six and Jehoshaphat's in chapter 20. Commentators often point to Jehoshaphat's prayer as a model prayer. He began with adoration of God, reminded him of his promises, set forth a problem, and asked for help. Confident, Jehoshaphat thanked God for the answer even before it came. We can use these prayers in the Bible as models for our own.

PRIORITIES

Do not worry, saying, 'What shall we eat?' or 'What shall we drink?' or 'What shall we wear?'... Seek first God's kingdom and his righteousness, and all these things will be given to you as well.

Matthew 6:31, 33

By faith Moses, when he had grown up, refused to be known as the son of Pharaoh's daughter. He chose to be mistreated along with the people of God rather than to enjoy the pleasures of sin for a short time. He regarded disgrace for the sake of Christ as of greater value than the treasures of Egypt, because he was looking ahead to his reward.

Hebrews 11:24–26

One of the Pharisees, an expert in the law, tested Jesus with this question: "Teacher, which is the greatest commandment in the Law?" Jesus replied: "'Love the Lord your God with all your heart and with all your soul and with all your mind.' This is the first and greatest commandment. And the second is like it: 'Love your neighbor as yourself.' All the Law and the Prophets hang on these two commandments."

Matthew 22:35–40

PRIORITIES

Jesus said, "Be faithful . . . and I will give you the crown of life."

Revelation 2:10

We fix our eyes not on what is seen, but on what is unseen. For what is seen is temporary, but what is unseen is eternal.

2 Corinthians 4:18

Let us not love with words or tongue but with actions and in truth.

1 John 3:18

If it is possible, as far as it depends on you, live at peace with everyone.

Romans 12:18

Imitate those who through faith and patience inherit what has been promised.

Hebrews 6:12

PRIORITIES

I consider my life worth nothing to me, if only I may finish the race and complete the task the Lord Jesus has given me—the task of testifying to the gospel of God's grace.

Acts 20:24

Make my joy complete by being like-minded, having the same love, being one in spirit and purpose. Do nothing out of selfish ambition or vain conceit, but in humility consider others better than yourselves. Each of you should look not only to your own interests, but also to the interests of others. Your attitude should be the same as that of Christ Jesus.

Philippians 2:2–5

Whatever you do, work at it with all your heart, as working for the Lord, not for men, since you know that you will receive an inheritance from the Lord as a reward. It is the Lord Christ you are serving.

Colossians 3:23–24

PRIORITIES

Deuteronomy is far from a rule book, although it repeats many of Israel's laws. A different spirit pervades it: the spirit of love. The rules in Deuteronomy read more like a guide on "How to Set Priorities for a Successful Life" than, say, an automobile maintenance manual. To keep up a car, you need only follow the rules. To maintain a close personal relationship, you need more—you need love.

Deuteronomy focuses on our motives: *why* people should obey laws. Again and again this book refers to the love of God for his people. In return God asks for obedience based on love, not on a sense of duty. At least fifteen times in Deuteronomy Moses tells the Israelites to love God and cling to him. God wants not just outward conformity but an obedience that comes from the heart.

Later, in summing up the Old Testament, Jesus quoted the first and greatest commandment from Deuteronomy: "Love the Lord your God with all your heart and with all your soul and with all your mind" (Matthew 22:37; Deuteronomy 6:5). That is our highest priority —to love God.

PROTECTION

You are my hiding place, O LORD;
you will protect me from trouble
and surround me with songs of deliverance.

Psalm 32:7

"When you pass through the waters,
I will be with you;
and when you pass through the rivers,
they will not sweep over you.
When you walk through the fire,
you will not be burned;
the flames will not set you ablaze,"
declares the LORD.

Isaiah 43:2

May the LORD answer you when you are in distress;
may the name of the God of Jacob protect you.
May he send you help from the sanctuary
and grant you support from Zion.

Psalm 20:1–2

God will command his angels concerning you
to guard you in all your ways.

Psalm 91:11

PROTECTION

"Because he loves me," says the LORD, "I will rescue him;
   I will protect him, for he acknowledges my name.
He will call upon me, and I will answer him;
   I will be with him in trouble,
   I will deliver him and honor him.
With long life will I satisfy him
   and show him my salvation."

                              Psalm 91:14–16

Jesus prayed, "Father, I have revealed you to
those whom you gave me out of the world.
They were yours; you gave them to me and they
have obeyed your word. . . . I will remain in the
world no longer, but they are still in the world,
and I am coming to you. Holy Father, protect
them by the power of your name—the name
you gave me—so that they may be one as we
are one."

                              John 17:6, 11

Let all who take refuge in you be glad, O LORD;
   let them ever sing for joy.
Spread your protection over them,
   that those who love your name may rejoice in you.

                              Psalm 5:11

PROTECTION

The Lord is faithful, and he will strengthen and protect you from the evil one.

2 Thessalonians 3:3

The LORD loves the just
 and will not forsake his faithful ones.
They will be protected forever.

Psalm 37:28

Whoever listens to wisdom will live in safety
 and be at ease, without fear of harm.

Proverbs 1:33

The eternal God is your refuge,
 and underneath are the everlasting arms.

Deuteronomy 33:27

PROTECTION

The book of Esther shows, though indirectly, God's heroic concern and protection for the Jews. The story runs on a series of extraordinary coincidences. Esther just "happened" to be chosen as the new queen. The king just "happened" to be unable to sleep, and, when he picked up some reading, just "happened" across an account of a good deed Esther's cousin Mordecai had done. The evil Haman just "happened" along at that crucial moment. These coincidences tilted terrible events toward the Jews' favor.

In the book of Esther God is not mentioned once and sometimes seems deliberately left out. But believing readers can have no doubt. All of life is under God's command. Nothing just happens. These "coincidences" were part of God's plan to save the Jews.

God protected his people because he loved them—because he had chosen them from the beginning. Esther's story is another chapter in the amazing story of God's perpetual love for the Jews. Though sometimes far from his will, this tiny, often hated minority has survived and thrived down the centuries.

RELATIONSHIP

Be kind and compassionate to one another, forgiving each other, just as in Christ God forgave you.

Ephesians 4:32

Respect those who work hard among you, who are over you in the Lord and who admonish you. Hold them in the highest regard in love because of their work. Live in peace with each other.

1 Thessalonians 5:12–13

Jesus said, "I no longer call you servants, because a servant does not know his master's business. Instead, I have called you friends, for everything that I learned from my Father I have made known to you."

John 15:15

Love your neighbor as yourself.

Matthew 22:39

Jesus said, "Whatever you did for one of the least of these brothers of mine, you did for me."

Matthew 25:40

Jesus said, "You have heard that it was said, 'Love your neighbor and hate your enemy.' But I tell you: Love your enemies and pray for those who persecute you, that you may be sons of your Father in heaven."

Matthew 5:43–45

Carry each other's burdens, and in this way you will fulfill the law of Christ. . . . Therefore, as we have opportunity, let us do good to all people, especially to those who belong to the family of believers.

Galatians 6:2, 10

Jesus said, "By this all men will know that you are my disciples, if you love one another."

John 13:35

RELATIONSHIP

Live in harmony with one another; be sympathetic, love as brothers, be compassionate and humble. Do not repay evil with evil or insult with insult, but with blessing, because to this you were called so that you may inherit a blessing.

1 Peter 3:8–9

There is a friend who sticks closer than a brother.

Proverbs 18:24

Dear friends, let us love one another, for love comes from God. Everyone who loves has been born of God and knows God.

1 John 4:7

He who walks with the wise grows wise.

Proverbs 13:20

How good and pleasant it is
    when brothers live together in unity!

Psalm 133:1

RELATIONSHIP

Mary Magdalene is an excellent example of a loving, faithful friend. All we know from the Bible's account of her life is that she came from Magdala, a city on the Sea of Galilee, and that Jesus drove seven demons from her. Having been healed by him, she dedicated her life to Jesus, her Savior and friend.

The Gospels, which focus on Jesus' twelve disciples, also mention that a good-sized crowd of women left their homes and families to follow Jesus (Matthew 27:55–56). Mary Magdalene heads the list of the women who helped finance his ministry.

When Jesus was crucified in Jerusalem, far from his home in Galilee, Mary Magdalene stayed near him. She carefully observed where he was buried and faithfully went there at the earliest opportunity to care for his body. As a result, she was the very first person to see Jesus risen from the dead and the first to spread the word (John 20:18).

REST

Let the beloved of the LORD rest secure in him,
  for he shields him all day long,
  and the one the LORD loves rests
    between his shoulders.

Deuteronomy 33:12

In repentance and rest is your salvation,
  in quietness and trust is your strength.

Isaiah 30:15

"I will refresh the weary and satisfy the faint,"
says the LORD.

Jeremiah 31:25

My soul finds rest in God alone;
  my salvation comes from him.

Psalm 62:1

He who dwells in the shelter of the Most High
  will rest in the shadow of the Almighty.

Psalm 91:1

We do not lose heart. Though outwardly we
are wasting away, yet inwardly we are being
renewed day by day.

2 Corinthians 4:16

REST

Jesus said, "Come to me, all you who are weary and burdened, and I will give you rest. Take my yoke upon you and learn from me, for I am gentle and humble in heart, and you will find rest for your souls. For my yoke is easy and my burden is light."

Matthew 11:28–30

Six days you shall labor and do all your work, but the seventh day is a Sabbath to the LORD your God. On it you shall not do any work.

Deuteronomy 5:13–14

I *have set the* LORD *always before me.*
   Because he is at my right hand,
   I will not be shaken.
Therefore my heart is glad and my tongue rejoices;
   my body also will rest secure.

Psalm 16:8–9

REST

This is what the LORD says:
"Stand at the crossroads and look;
ask for the ancient paths,
ask where the good way is, and walk in it,
and you will find rest for your souls."

Jeremiah 6:16

There remains . . . a Sabbath-rest for the people of God; for anyone who enters God's rest also rests from his own work, just as God did from his.

Hebrews 4:9–10

Because so many people were coming and going that [the disciples] did not even have a chance to eat, Jesus said to them, "Come with me by yourselves to a quiet place and get some rest."

Mark 6:31

The LORD your God is with you,
he is mighty to save.
He will take great delight in you,
he will quiet you with his love,
he will rejoice over you with singing.

Zephaniah 3:17

The *fear of the* LORD *leads to life*:
   Then one rests content, untouched by trouble.

                                   Proverbs 19:23

Be at rest once more, O my soul,
   for the LORD *has been good to you.*

                                   Psalm 116:7

Praise be to the LORD, who has given rest to his
people Israel just as he promised.

                                   1 Kings 8:56

Preserve sound judgment and discernment,
   do not let them out of your sight;
they will be life for you,
   an ornament to grace your neck.
Then you will go on your way in safety,
   and your foot will not stumble;
when you lie down, you will not be afraid;
   when you lie down, your sleep will be sweet.

                                   Proverbs 3:21–24

I will lie down and sleep in peace,
   for you alone, O LORD,
   make me dwell in safety.

                                   Psalm 4:8

REST

The LORD is my shepherd, I shall not be in want.
  He makes me lie down in green pastures,
he leads me beside quiet waters,
  he restores my soul.
He guides me in paths of righteousness
  for his name's sake.
Even though I walk
  through the valley of the shadow of death,
I will fear no evil,
  for you are with me;
your rod and your staff,
  they comfort me.
You prepare a table before me
  in the presence of my enemies.
You anoint my head with oil;
  my cup overflows.
Surely goodness and love will follow me
  all the days of my life,
and I will dwell in the house of the LORD
  forever.

Psalm 23

REST

Mark graphically shows the press of the crowds around Jesus. Wherever he went, people followed, bringing him the sick to heal and challenging him with questions. In five separate places (Mark 3:7–9; 6:31; 6:45; 7:24; 9:30) Mark records that Jesus took his disciples aside to some quiet place to escape the crush of the crowd.

In addition Jesus spent quiet time alone, away from even his disciples, to gain rest and strength for his ministry. Mark records that Jesus got up "very early in the morning, while it was still dark" (Mark 1:35) to pray by himself. This pattern of quiet time is a good example for us to follow as well. We need rest in the Lord, away from other people and pressing concerns, for our bodies as well as for our minds.

SHARING YOUR FAITH

I am not ashamed of the gospel, because it is the power of God for the salvation of everyone who believes: first for the Jew, then for the Gentile. For in the gospel a righteousness from God is revealed, a righteousness that is by faith from first to last, just as it is written: "The righteous will live by faith."

Romans 1:16–17

Thanks be to God, who always leads us in triumphal procession in Christ and through us spreads everywhere the fragrance of the knowledge of him.

2 Corinthians 2:14

God so loved the world that he gave his one and only Son, that whoever believes in him shall not perish but have eternal life. For God did not send his Son into the world to condemn the world, but to save the world through him.

John 3:16–17

Jesus said to his disciples, "Go into all the world and preach the good news to all creation."

Mark 16:15

"Now go; I will help you speak and will teach you what to say," said the LORD.

Exodus 4:12

SHARING YOUR FAITH

Let your light shine before men, that they may see your good deeds and praise your Father in heaven.

Matthew 5:16

"Come, follow me," Jesus said, "and I will make you fishers of men."

Matthew 4:19

The disciples went out and preached everywhere, and the Lord worked with them and confirmed his word by the signs that accompanied it.

Mark 16:20

When Jesus had called the Twelve together, he gave them power and authority to drive out all demons and to cure diseases, and he sent them out to preach the kingdom of God and to heal the sick. . . . So they set out and went from village to village, preaching the gospel and healing people everywhere.

Luke 9:1–2, 6

One night the Lord spoke to Paul in a vision: "Do not be afraid; keep on speaking, do not be silent. For I am with you, and no one is going to attack and harm you."

Acts 18:9–10

SHARING YOUR FAITH

I always thank my God as I remember you in my prayers, because I hear about your faith in the Lord Jesus and your love for all the saints. I pray that you may be active in sharing your faith, so that you will have a full understanding of every good thing we have in Christ.

Philemon 4–6

I consider my life worth nothing to me, if only I may finish the race and complete the task the Lord Jesus has given me—the task of testifying to the gospel of God's grace.

Acts 20:24

Jesus said, "The Counselor, the Holy Spirit, whom the Father will send in my name, will teach you all things and will remind you of everything I have said to you."

John 14:26

We do not preach ourselves, but Jesus Christ as Lord, and ourselves as your servants for Jesus' sake. For God, who said, "Let light shine out of darkness," made his light shine in our hearts to give us the light of the knowledge of the glory of God in the face of Christ. But we have this treasure in jars of clay to show that this all-surpassing power is from God and not from us.

2 Corinthians 4:5–7

SHARING YOUR FAITH

Where would you keep expensive jewelry? You would want a safe, secure place. You wouldn't stash valuables in, say, a tattered cardboard box. Yet this image comes close to the one Paul used to describe his ministry: "jars of clay." In his day jars were about as common—and as safe—as cardboard boxes are today.

The treasure Paul refers to in 2 Corinthians 4:7 is the incredible message of the gospel: God's good news of forgiveness and the promise of life forever. Yet, amazingly, God chose to enclose that treasure in people who are like "jars of clay." Clay jars are ordinary and highly breakable, and Paul tells us he is both. An immortal God chooses mere humans as his personal representatives.

You are like a clay jar too, not perfect and maybe pretty ordinary, but God has chosen to give you the precious treasure of his gospel to share with people around you.

STRENGTH

"Do not fear, for I am with you;
   do not be dismayed, for I am your God.
I will strengthen you and help you;
   I will uphold you with my righteous right hand,"
      declares the LORD.

Isaiah 41:10

"My hand will sustain him;
   surely my arm will strengthen him,"
says the LORD.

Psalm 89:21

The LORD will guide you always;
   he will satisfy your needs in a sun-scorched land
   and will strengthen your frame.
You will be like a well-watered garden,
   like a spring whose waters never fail.

Isaiah 58:11

"I will search for the lost and bring back the strays. I will bind up the injured and strengthen the weak," declares the LORD.

Ezekiel 34:16

STRENGTH

The eyes of the LORD range throughout the earth to strengthen those whose hearts are fully committed to him.

2 Chronicles 16:9

I pray that out of God's glorious riches he may strengthen you with power through his Spirit in your inner being, so that Christ may dwell in your hearts through faith.

Ephesians 3:16–17

May our Lord Jesus Christ himself and God our Father, who loved us and by his grace gave us eternal encouragement and good hope, encourage your hearts and strengthen you in every good deed and word.

2 Thessalonians 2:16–17

The Lord is faithful, and he will strengthen and protect you from the evil one.

2 Thessalonians 3:3

The LORD is my strength and my song;
he has become my salvation.
He is my God, and I will praise him,
my father's God, and I will exalt him.

Exodus 15:2

167

STRENGTH

It is God who arms me with strength
and makes my way perfect.

2 Samuel 22:33

Do not grieve, for the joy of the LORD is your strength.

Nehemiah 8:10

The LORD gives strength to his people;
the LORD blesses his people with peace.

Psalm 29:11

The LORD is my strength and my shield;
my heart trusts in him, and I am helped.
My heart leaps for joy
and I will give thanks to him in song.
The LORD is the strength of his people,
a fortress of salvation for his anointed one.

Psalm 28:7–8

The Lord stood at my side and gave me strength, so that through me the message might be fully proclaimed and all the Gentiles might hear it.

2 Timothy 4:17

I thank Christ Jesus our Lord, who has given me strength, that he considered me faithful, appointing me to his service.

1 Timothy 1:12

God is our refuge and strength,
an ever-present help in trouble.

Psalm 46:1

I can do everything through Christ who gives me strength.

Philippians 4:13

The God of all grace, who called you to his eternal glory in Christ, after you have suffered a little while, will himself restore you and make you strong, firm and steadfast.

1 Peter 5:10

If anyone speaks, he should do it as one speaking the very words of God. If anyone serves, he should do it with the strength God provides, so that in all things God may be praised through Jesus Christ. To him be the glory and the power for ever and ever.

1 Peter 4:11

STRENGTH

Do you not know?
  Have you not heard?
The LORD is the everlasting God,
  the Creator of the ends of the earth.
He will not grow tired or weary,
  and his understanding no one can fathom.
He gives strength to the weary
  and increases the power of the weak.
Even youths grow tired and weary,
  and young men stumble and fall;
but those who hope in the LORD
  will renew their strength.
They will soar on wings like eagles;
  they will run and not grow weary,
they will walk and not be faint.

Isaiah 40:28–31

STRENGTH

College sophomore Tom Bowers took a summer job as an intern on the governor of Michigan's staff. One day a harried manager asked Tom to write a public statement on the state's new law enforcement program. Tom composed a brief announcement and took it to the governor.

The next day he was stunned to see, headlined across the front page of the *Detroit News*, the announcement he had composed. It dawned on him that people would be reading his very own words as the governor's. Throughout that summer, Tom discovered the power of the governor's name.

It is one thing to represent the governor of Michigan; it is quite another to represent God and use his name. Yet Jesus had exactly that plan in mind for his followers. In the same way that a governor or president delegates authority to people acting on his behalf, Jesus gave his followers his own authority and power and strength.

The apostle Paul said that we, the church, actually form Christ's body in the world. Jesus called on his people to represent him—to carry his strength and power to the world. In every sense we bear his name.

STRESS

In my anguish I cried to the LORD,
and he answered by setting me free.

Psalm 118:5

Wait for the LORD;
be strong and take heart
and wait for the LORD.

Psalm 27:14

Find rest, O my soul, in God alone;
my hope comes from him.

Psalm 62:5

Those who hope in the LORD
will renew their strength.
They will soar on wings like eagles;
they will run and not grow weary,
they will walk and not be faint.

Isaiah 40:31

Let us hold unswervingly to the hope we
profess, for God who promised is faithful.

Hebrews 10:23

STRESS

The eyes of all look to you, O LORD,
    and you give them their food at the proper time.
You open your hand
    and satisfy the desires of every living thing.
The LORD is righteous in all his ways
    and loving toward all he has made.
The LORD is near to all who call on him,
    to all who call on him in truth.
He fulfills the desires of those who fear him;
    he hears their cry and saves them.

Psalm 145:15–19

An anxious heart weighs a man down,
    but a kind word cheers him up.

Proverbs 12:25

I wait for the LORD, my soul waits,
    and in his word I put my hope.

Psalm 130:5

You will keep in perfect peace
    him whose mind is steadfast,
    because he trusts in you, O LORD.

Isaiah 26:3

STRESS

Rejoice in the Lord always. I will say it again: Rejoice! Let your gentleness be evident to all. The Lord is near. Do not be anxious about anything, but in everything, by prayer and petition, with thanksgiving, present your requests to God. And the peace of God, which transcends all understanding, will guard your hearts and your minds in Christ Jesus.

Philippians 4:4–7

Surely this is our God;
we trusted in him, and he saved us.
This is the LORD, *we trusted in him;*
let us rejoice and be glad in his salvation.

Isaiah 25:9

Jesus said, "Peace I leave with you; my peace I give you. I do not give to you as the world gives. Do not let your hearts be troubled and do not be afraid."

John 14:27

STRESS

How could it happen? All at once the world came crashing down on a single innocent man named Job. It was the ultimate in unfairness. First raiders stole his belongings and slaughtered his servants. Then fire from the sky burned up his sheep, and a mighty wind destroyed his house and killed his sons and daughters. Finally Job came down with a horrible, painful disease. "What did I do to deserve such suffering?" he wailed.

Like all grieving and stressed-out people, Job went through emotional cycles. He whined, exploded, cajoled, and collapsed into self-pity. He agreed with his friends, then shifted positions and contradicted himself. And occasionally he came up with a statement of brilliant hope.

Sooner or later we all find ourselves in a position somewhat like Job's. Our world seems to crumble. Nothing makes sense anymore. God seems distant and silent.

At such moments of great crisis and stress, Job's life stands as an example to us. And we can be thankful that he came through it, as we will, with great blessings afterward.

TALENTS AND ABILITIES

We are God's workmanship, created in Christ Jesus to do good works, which God prepared in advance for us to do.

Ephesians 2:10

God's gifts and his call are irrevocable.

Romans 11:29

God gives wisdom to the wise and knowledge to the discerning.

Daniel 2:21

Whatever you do, work at it with all your heart, as working for the Lord, not for men, since you know that you will receive an inheritance from the Lord as a reward. It is the Lord Christ you are serving.

Colossians 3:23–24

Since you are eager to have spiritual gifts, try to excel in gifts that build up the church.

1 Corinthians 14:12

Skill will bring success.

Ecclesiastes 10:10

TALENTS AND ABILITIES

There are different kinds of gifts, but the same Spirit. . . . Now to each one the manifestation of the Spirit is given for the common good. To one there is given through the Spirit the message of wisdom, to another the message of knowledge by means of the same Spirit, to another faith by the same Spirit, to another gifts of healing by that one Spirit, to another miraculous powers, to another prophecy, to another distinguishing between spirits, to another speaking in different kinds of tongues, and to still another the interpretation of tongues. All these are the work of one and the same Spirit, and he gives them to each one, just as he determines.

1 Corinthians 12:4, 7–11

Never be lacking in zeal, but keep your spiritual fervor, serving the Lord.

Romans 12:11

It is the spirit in a man, the breath of the Almighty, that gives him understanding.

Job 32:8

We have different gifts, according to the grace given us. If a man's gift is prophesying, let him use it in proportion to his faith. If it is serving, let him serve; if it is teaching, let him teach; if it is encouraging, let him encourage; if it is contributing to the needs of others, let him give generously; if it is leadership, let him govern diligently; if it is showing mercy, let him do it cheerfully.

Romans 12:6–8

Every good and perfect gift is from above, coming down from the Father of the heavenly lights, who does not change like shifting shadows.

James 1:17

TALENTS AND ABILITIES

Today when we speak of a "talented" musician or athlete, we are actually harking back to the parable of the talents recorded in Matthew 25. A talent in Jesus' time was a valuable sum of money worth about two years' wages. Because of this parable, the word acquired a different meaning. Each person in the kingdom of heaven is given a certain number of gifts and opportunities ("talents") to serve God. We can either waste those opportunities or invest them in a way that furthers the kingdom.

We need to use our abilities to build up the church. In First Corinthians 12, Paul gives a clever anatomy lesson, with a purpose. By comparing members of the church of Christ to parts of a human body, he neatly explains two complementary truths. Any part of a body, he says—such as an eye or a foot—with its unique abilities, makes a valuable contribution to the whole body. Whenever a single member is missing, the entire body suffers. And, he continues, no member can survive if isolated from the rest. Alone, an eye is useless. All parts and all abilities must cooperate to form a single, unified body.

TEMPTATION

Consider it pure joy, ... whenever you face trials of many kinds, because you know that the testing of your faith develops perseverance. Perseverance must finish its work so that you may be mature and complete, not lacking anything.

James 1:2–4

Jesus prayed,
"Lead us not into temptation,
    but deliver us from the evil one."

Matthew 6:13

Submit yourselves ... to God. Resist the devil, and he will flee from you. Come near to God and he will come near to you.

James 4:7–8

The Lord knows how to rescue godly men from trials.

2 Peter 2:9

We do not have a high priest who is unable to sympathize with our weaknesses, but we have one who has been tempted in every way, just as we are—yet was without sin. Let us then approach the throne of grace with confidence, so that we may receive mercy and find grace to help us in our time of need.

Hebrews 4:15–16

TEMPTATION

No temptation has seized you except what is common to man. And God is faithful; he will not let you be tempted beyond what you can bear. But when you are tempted, he will also provide a way out so that you can stand up under it.

1 Corinthians 10:13

Be strong in the Lord and in his mighty power. Put on the full armor of God so that you can take your stand against the devil's schemes. For our struggle is not against flesh and blood, but against the rulers, against the authorities, against the powers of this dark world and against the spiritual forces of evil in the heavenly realms. Therefore put on the full armor of God, so that when the day of evil comes, you may be able to stand your ground, and after you have done everything, to stand. Stand firm then, with the belt of truth buckled around your waist, with the breastplate of righteousness in place, and with your feet fitted with the readiness that comes from the gospel of peace. In addition to all this, take up the shield of faith, with which you can extinguish all the flaming arrows of the evil one. Take the helmet of salvation and the sword of the Spirit, which is the word of God.

Ephesians 6:10–17

TEMPTATION

Because Jesus himself suffered when he was tempted, he is able to help those who are being tempted.

Hebrews 2:18

The weapons we fight with are not the weapons of the world. On the contrary, they have divine power to demolish strongholds. We demolish arguments and every pretension that sets itself up against the knowledge of God, and we take captive every thought to make it obedient to Christ.

2 Corinthians 10:4–5

If we confess our sins, God is faithful and just and will forgive us our sins and purify us from all unrighteousness.

1 John 1:9

Dear friends, do not believe every spirit, but test the spirits to see whether they are from God, because many false prophets have gone out into the world. . . . You, dear children, are from God and have overcome them, because the one who is in you is greater than the one who is in the world.

1 John 4:1, 4

TEMPTATION

When tempted by Satan (Luke 4:1–13), Jesus responded with three separate quotations from Deuteronomy: Deuteronomy 8:3 and 6:13, 16. In the desert, the Israelites had learned that God would provide all they needed. Jesus, also in the desert, quoted Scripture to forcefully remind Satan of that lesson. We too can trust God to provide even when we are tempted to believe otherwise.

James's call for joy in the face of trials and temptations may seem shocking or even insensitive at first (James 1:2–4). A close reading, though, makes clear that James finds joy in the results of the trials, not in the trials themselves. Even difficult times can produce good qualities.

Jude concludes triumphantly that when we are tempted, God is able to keep us from falling (Jude 24).

GOD'S WORDS OF LIFE ON
TRUST

Trust in the LORD and do good;
    dwell in the land and enjoy safe pasture.
Delight yourself in the LORD
    and he will give you the desires of your heart.
Commit your way to the LORD;
    trust in him and he will do this:
He will make your righteousness shine like the dawn,
    the justice of your cause like the noonday sun.

Psalm 37:3–6

Those who know your name will trust in you,
    for you, LORD, have never forsaken those
who seek you.

Psalm 9:10

Blessed is the man who trusts in the LORD,
    whose confidence is in him.

Jeremiah 17:7

Trust in the LORD with all your heart
    and lean not on your own understanding;
in all your ways acknowledge him,
    and he will make your paths straight.

Proverbs 3:5–6

Trust in the LORD at all times, O people;
  pour out your hearts to him,
  for God is our refuge.

Psalm 62:8

May the God of hope fill you with all joy
and peace as you trust in him, so that you
may overflow with hope by the power of the
Holy Spirit.

Romans 15:13

Surely God is my salvation;
  I will trust and not be afraid.
The LORD, the LORD, is my strength and my song;
  he has become my salvation.

Isaiah 12:2

Some trust in chariots and some in horses,
  but we trust in the name of the LORD our God.

Psalm 20:7

Those who trust in the LORD are like Mount Zion,
  which cannot be shaken but endures forever.

Psalm 125:1

TRUST

Surely this is our God;
   we trusted in him, and he saved us.
This is the LORD, we trusted in him;
   let us rejoice and be glad in his salvation.

Isaiah 25:9

When I am afraid,
   I will trust in you, O LORD.
In God, whose word I praise,
   in God I trust; I will not be afraid.
   What can mortal man do to me?

Psalm 56:3–4

Let the morning bring me word of your
   unfailing love, O LORD,
   for I have put my trust in you.
Show me the way I should go,
   for to you I lift up my soul.

Psalm 143:8

Whoever gives heed to instruction prospers,
   and blessed is he who trusts in the LORD.

Proverbs 16:20

TRUST

The LORD God is a sun and shield;
   the LORD bestows favor and honor;
no good thing does he withhold
   from those whose walk is blameless.
O LORD Almighty,
   blessed is the man who trusts in you.

Psalm 84:11–12

"See, I lay a stone in Zion,
   a chosen and precious cornerstone,
and the one who trusts in him
   will never be put to shame," declares the Lord.

1 Peter 2:6

The LORD is my strength and my shield;
   my heart trusts in him, and I am helped.
My heart leaps for joy
   and I will give thanks to him in song.

Psalm 28:7

I am not ashamed, because I know whom I have
believed, and am convinced that God is able to
guard what I have entrusted to him.

2 Timothy 1:12

GOD'S WORDS OF LIFE ON
TRUST

Here is a trustworthy saying that deserves full acceptance: Christ Jesus came into the world to save sinners.

1 Timothy 1:15

Love always protects, always trusts, always hopes, always perseveres.

1 Corinthians 13:7

Jesus said, "Do not let your hearts be troubled. Trust in God; trust also in me."

John 14:1

In quietness and trust is your strength.

Isaiah 30:15

TRUST

The author of Hebrews wrote to people who faced a climactic, can't-turn-back decision that involved their entire future. Should they stick with their familiar routine of the Jewish religion, trusting in their laws to save them? Or should they take a risk and join the growing body of people who called themselves Christians, trusting in Jesus as their Savior? The book of Hebrews seems designed to push such people toward a decisive commitment. Point by point, the author shows how Christ improved on the Jewish way and the Jewish laws.

Look at it this way: Buy two identical plants in a nursery. Plant one in a desert and one by a river. For a few days they'll look alike, but what happens after a few weeks? That's the image Jeremiah uses in Jeremiah 17:5–8. The person who trusts in humans or in human efforts for salvation will end up like a shriveled bush (verse 6), while the person who trusts God will be like a tree that has its roots sunk deep beside a stream (verse 8).

WISDOM

I keep asking that the God of our Lord Jesus Christ, the glorious Father, may give you the Spirit of wisdom and revelation, so that you may know him better.

Ephesians 1:17

To God belong wisdom and power;
counsel and understanding are his.

Job 12:13

Oh, the depth of the riches of the wisdom
and knowledge of God!
How unsearchable his judgments,
and his paths beyond tracing out!

Romans 11:33

Wisdom is a shelter
as money is a shelter,
but the advantage of knowledge is this:
that wisdom preserves the life of its possessor.

Ecclesiastes 7:12

The mouth of the righteous man utters wisdom,
and his tongue speaks what is just.

Psalm 37:30

WISDOM

This is what the LORD says, he who made the earth, the LORD who formed it and established it—the LORD is his name: "Call to me and I will answer you and tell you great and unsearchable things you do not know."

Jeremiah 33:2–3

Wisdom is supreme; therefore get wisdom.
Though it cost all you have, get understanding.

Proverbs 4:7

Surely you desire truth in the inner parts, O LORD;
you teach me wisdom in the inmost place.

Psalm 51:6

The fear of the LORD is the beginning of wisdom,
and knowledge of the Holy One is understanding.

Proverbs 9:10

Listen to advice and accept instruction,
and in the end you will be wise.

Proverbs 19:20

He who gets wisdom loves his own soul;
he who cherishes understanding prospers.

Proverbs 19:8

WISDOM

My son, if you accept my words
    and store up my commands within you,
turning your ear to wisdom
    and applying your heart to understanding,
and if you call out for insight
    and cry aloud for understanding,
and if you look for it as for silver
    and search for it as for hidden treasure,
then you will understand the fear of the LORD
    and find the knowledge of God.

Proverbs 2:1–5

Blessed is the man who finds wisdom,
    the man who gains understanding,
for she is more profitable than silver
    and yields better returns than gold.

Proverbs 3:13–14

By wisdom a house is built,
    and through understanding it is established;
through knowledge its rooms are filled
    with rare and beautiful treasures.

Proverbs 24:3–4

A *man's wisdom gives him patience;*
it is to his glory to overlook an offense.

Proverbs 19:11

If any of you lacks wisdom, he should ask God, who gives generously to all without finding fault, and it will be given to him.

James 1:5

The fruit of the righteous is a tree of life,
and he who wins souls is wise.

Proverbs 11:30

The teaching of the wise is a fountain of life,
turning a man from the snares of death.

Proverbs 13:14

Jesus said, "Everyone who hears these words of mine and puts them into practice is like a wise man who built his house on the rock. The rain came down, the streams rose, and the winds blew and beat against that house; yet it did not fall, because it had its foundation on the rock."

Matthew 7:24–25

WISDOM

Where can wisdom be found?
  Where does understanding dwell?
Man does not comprehend its worth;
  it cannot be found in the land of the living.
The deep says, "It is not in me";
  the sea says, "It is not with me."
It cannot be bought with the finest gold,
  nor can its price be weighed in silver. . . .
Neither gold nor crystal can compare with it,
  nor can it be had for jewels of gold.
Coral and jasper are not worthy of mention;
  the price of wisdom is beyond rubies. . . .
Where then does wisdom come from?
  Where does understanding dwell?
It is hidden from the eyes of every living thing,
  concealed even from the birds of the air. . . .
God understands the way to it
  and he alone knows where it dwells,
for he views the ends of the earth
  and sees everything under the heavens.

Job 28:12–15, 17–18, 20–21, 23–24

WISDOM

Proverbs judges every thought or action by one standard: "Is this wise?" The word *wisdom* brings up pictures of gray-haired old men muttering obscure philosophic maxims. But that is almost the opposite of what Proverbs means by the word. Wisdom is above all practical and down-to-earth. Young people as well as old can and should have it. Wisdom teaches you how to live. It combines understanding with discipline—the kind of discipline an athlete needs in training. It also adds a healthy dose of good common sense—except that common sense isn't, and never has been, common.

How do you become a wise person? You must first begin to listen. Wisdom is freely available to those who will stop talking and start paying attention—to God and his Word, to parents, to wise counselors. Anybody can become wise, Proverbs says. Wisdom is not reserved for a brainy elite. But becoming wise requires self-discipline to study and humbly seek wisdom at every opportunity.

WORDS

May the words of my mouth and the meditation
     of my heart
     be pleasing in your sight,
     O LORD, my Rock and my Redeemer.

> Psalm 19:14

My mouth will speak words of wisdom;
     the utterance from my heart will give understanding.

> Psalm 49:3

The wise in heart are called discerning,
     and pleasant words promote instruction.

> Proverbs 16:21

Pleasant words are a honeycomb,
     sweet to the soul and healing to the bones.

> Proverbs 16:24

A man of knowledge uses words with restraint,
     and a man of understanding is even-tempered.

> Proverbs 17:27

Gold there is, and rubies in abundance,
     but lips that speak knowledge are a rare jewel.

> Proverbs 20:15

He who loves a pure heart and whose speech is gracious
   will have the king for his friend.

Proverbs 22:11

"Have faith in God," Jesus [said]. "I tell you
the truth, if anyone says to this mountain,
'Go, throw yourself into the sea,' and does
not doubt in his heart but believes that what
he says will happen, it will be done for him."

Mark 11:22–23

How sweet are your words to my taste, O LORD,
   sweeter than honey to my mouth!

Psalm 119:103

Whoever would love life
   and see good days
must keep his tongue from evil
   and his lips from deceitful speech.

1 Peter 3:10

The tongue that brings healing is a tree of life.

Proverbs 15:4

WORDS

A *man finds joy in giving an apt reply—*
and how good is a timely word!

Proverbs 15:23

If you confess with your mouth, "Jesus is Lord,"
and believe in your heart that God raised him
from the dead, you will be saved. For it is with
your heart that you believe and are justified,
and it is with your mouth that you confess and
are saved.

Romans 10:9–10

He *who guards his mouth and his tongue*
keeps himself from calamity.

Proverbs 21:23

DEVOTIONAL THOUGHT ON

WORDS

What could be wrong with just talking, as long as you don't actually lie? Proverbs sees plenty of danger. Words are dynamite; they can destroy people. They should be carefully weighed before they are spoken. Even truthful words can damage. Yet they can also save a friend from going wrong. Proverbs speaks strongly about both the danger of gossip and the good done when someone justly rebukes his or her friend.

"The tongue has the power of life and death," Proverbs 18:21 says, "and those who love it will eat its fruit." Proverbs teaches the skill of speaking so as to give life.

WORK

Whatever you do, whether in word or deed, do it all in the name of the Lord Jesus, giving thanks to God the Father through him.

Colossians 3:17

Whatever your hand finds to do, do it with all your might.

Ecclesiastes 9:10

If you fully obey the LORD your God . . . the LORD will open the heavens, the storehouse of his bounty, to send rain on your land in season and to bless all the work of your hands. You will lend to many nations but will borrow from none.

Deuteronomy 28:1, 12

God is not unjust; he will not forget your work and the love you have shown him as you have helped his people and continue to help them. We want each of you to show this same diligence to the very end, in order to make your hope sure. We do not want you to become lazy, but to imitate those who through faith and patience inherit what has been promised.

Hebrews 6:10–12

Diligent hands will rule.

Proverbs 12:24

Six days you shall labor, but on the seventh day you shall rest.

Exodus 34:21

May the favor of the Lord our God rest upon us;
  establish the work of our hands for us—
  yes, establish the work of our hands.

Psalm 90:17

From the fruit of his lips a man is filled with good things
  as surely as the work of his hands rewards him.

Proverbs 12:14

All hard work brings a profit.

Proverbs 14:23

Whatever you do, work at it with all your heart, as working for the Lord, not for men, since you know that you will receive an inheritance from the Lord as a reward.

Colossians 3:23–24

He who works his land will have abundant food.

Proverbs 12:11

WORK

The desires of the diligent are fully satisfied.

Proverbs 13:4

Jesus said, "Take my yoke upon you and learn from me, for I am gentle and humble in heart, and you will find rest for your souls. For my yoke is easy and my burden is light."

Matthew 11:29–30

Jesus said, "My Father is always at his work to this very day, and I, too, am working."

John 5:17

The sleep of a laborer is sweet,
whether he eats little or much.

Ecclesiastes 5:12

Do your best to present yourself to God as one approved, a workman who does not need to be ashamed and who correctly handles the word of truth.

2 Timothy 2:15

WORK

Paul's first letter to the Thessalonians affirmed that Jesus could return at any time, unexpectedly. Evidently, this anticipation prompted some to quit their jobs and do nothing but wait for the Second Coming. To correct the imbalance, in the second letter to Thessalonica, Paul stressed that certain events must happen before Christ's return. He also strongly warned against idleness, telling people it is good to continue working.

Similarly, the Israelites grew tired of their calling (see Ezekiel 20). They wanted to relax, stop working so hard, and live like other nations. But God swore he would never let it happen. He would remain strict, even putting them through another desert experience to purify them, but he absolutely refused to let them conform. God is pleased with honest, hard work rather than idleness.

WORRY

Do not be anxious about anything, but in everything, by prayer and petition, with thanksgiving, present your requests to God. And the peace of God, which transcends all understanding, will guard your hearts and your minds in Christ Jesus.

Philippians 4:6–7

When anxiety was great within me, O LORD,
your consolation brought joy to my soul.

Psalm 94:19

Jesus said, "I tell you, do not worry about your life, what you will eat or drink; or about your body, what you will wear. Is not life more important than food, and the body more important than clothes? Look at the birds of the air; they do not sow or reap or store away in barns, and yet your heavenly Father feeds them. Are you not much more valuable than they? Who of you by worrying can add a single hour to his life?"

Matthew 6:25–27

An anxious heart weighs a man down,
but a kind word cheers him up.

Proverbs 12:25

WORRY

Jesus said, "Why do you worry about clothes? See how the lilies of the field grow. They do not labor or spin. Yet I tell you that not even Solomon in all his splendor was dressed like one of these. If that is how God clothes the grass of the field, which is here today and tomorrow is thrown into the fire, will he not much more clothe you, O you of little faith? So do not worry, saying, 'What shall we eat?' or 'What shall we drink?' or 'What shall we wear?' For the pagans run after all these things, and your heavenly Father knows that you need them. But seek first his kingdom and his right-eousness, and all these things will be given to you as well. Therefore do not worry about tomorrow, for tomorrow will worry about itself."

Matthew 6:28–34

Be happy, young man, while you are young,
and let your heart give you joy in the
days of your youth. . . .
So then, banish anxiety from your heart
and cast off the troubles of your body.

Ecclesiastes 11:9–10

WORRY

Cast all your anxiety on God because he cares for you.

1 Peter 5:7

The LORD is my shepherd, I shall not be in want.
   He makes me lie down in green pastures,
he leads me beside quiet waters,
   he restores my soul.
He guides me in paths of righteousness
   for his name's sake.
Even though I walk
   through the valley of the shadow of death,
I will fear no evil,
   for you are with me;
your rod and your staff,
   they comfort me.

Psalm 23:1–4

Jesus said, "Do not let your hearts be troubled. Trust in God; trust also in me."

John 14:1

WORRY

We often worry about things like having enough money to pay the bills. In Luke 12:15–31 Jesus neatly summarized his usual approach to money. He did not condemn the possession of it, but he did warn against putting faith in money to secure the future. The rich man's money did him absolutely no good the night of his death. To emphasize his point, Jesus referred back to King Solomon, the richest man in the Old Testament. The lesson: Trust in God and his kingdom, and free yourself of worry about money and possessions.

We should not worry or be anxious but keep our eyes on God, who always takes care of us.

Look for other books in the God's Words of Life series:

God's Words of Life for Teens

God's Words of Life for Leaders

God's Words of Life from the Women's
      Devotional Bible 2

More of God's Words of Life for Women

God's Words of Life from the Men's
      Devotional Bible

God's Words of Life from the Classics
      Devotional Bible

God's Words of Life for Couples

God's Words of Life on Marriage

God's Words of Life for Moms

God's Words of Life for Dads